MW01034117

SECOND EDITION

Methods for Policy Research

APPLIED SOCIAL RESEARCH
METHODS SERIES

1. **SURVEY RESEARCH METHODS (Fourth Edition)**
   by FLOYD J. FOWLER, Jr.
2. **SYNTHESIZING RESEARCH (Third Edition)**
   by HARRIS COOPER
3. **METHODS FOR POLICY RESEARCH**
   (Second Edition)
   by ANN MAJCHRZAK and M. LYNNE MARKUS
4. **SECONDARY RESEARCH (Second Edition)**
   by DAVID W. STEWART and MICHAEL A. KAMINS
5. **CASE STUDY RESEARCH (Fifth Edition)**
   by ROBERT K. YIN
6. **META-ANALYTIC PROCEDURES FOR SOCIAL**
   RESEARCH (Revised Edition)
   by ROBERT ROSENTHAL
7. **TELEPHONE SURVEY METHODS (Second Edition)**
   by PAUL J. LAVRAKAS
8. **DIAGNOSING ORGANIZATIONS (Second Edition)**
   by MICHAEL I. HARRISON
9. **GROUP TECHNIQUES FOR**
   IDEA BUILDING (Second Edition)
   by CARL M. MOORE
10. **NEED ANALYSIS**
    by JACK McKILLIP
11. **LINKING AUDITING AND META EVALUATION**
    by THOMAS A. SCHWANDT
    and EDWARD S. HALPERN
12. **ETHICS AND VALUES**
    IN APPLIED SOCIAL RESEARCH
    by ALLAN J. KIMMEL
13. **ON TIME AND METHOD**
    by JANICE R. KELLY
    and JOSEPH E. McGRATH
14. **RESEARCH IN HEALTH CARE SETTINGS**
    by KATHLEEN E. GRADY
    and BARBARA STRUDLER WALLSTON
15. **PARTICIPANT OBSERVATION**
    by DANNY L. JORGENSEN
16. **INTERPRETIVE INTERACTIONISM (Second Edition)**
    by NORMAN K. DENZIN
17. **ETHNOGRAPHY (Third Edition)**
    by DAVID M. FETTERMAN
18. **STANDARDIZED SURVEY INTERVIEWING**
    by FLOYD J. FOWLER, Jr.,
    and THOMAS W. MANGIONE
19. **PRODUCTIVITY MEASUREMENT**
    by ROBERT O. BRINKERHOFF
    and DENNIS E. DRESSLER
20. **FOCUS GROUPS (Second Edition)**
    by DAVID W. STEWART,
    PREM N. SHAMDASANI, and DENNIS W. ROOK
21. **PRACTICAL SAMPLING**
    by GART T. HENRY
22. **DECISION RESEARCH**
    by JOHN S. CARROLL and ERIC J. JOHNSON
23. **RESEARCH WITH HISPANIC POPULATIONS**
    by GERARDO MARIN
    and BARBARA VANOSS MARIN
24. **INTERNAL EVALUATION**
    by ARNOLD J. LOVE
25. **COMPUTER SIMULATION APPLICATIONS**
    by MARCIA LYNN WHICKER and LEE SIGELMAN
26. **SCALE DEVELOPMENT (Third Edition)**
    by ROBERT F. DeVELLIS
27. **STUDYING FAMILIES**
    by ANNE P. COPELAND and KATHLEEN M. WHITE
28. **EVENT HISTORY ANALYSIS**
    by KAZUO YAMAGUCHI
29. **RESEARCH IN EDUCATIONAL SETTINGS**
    by GEOFFREY MARUYAMA
    and STANLEY DENO
30. **RESEARCHING PERSONS WITH**
    MENTAL ILLNESS
    by ROSALIND J. DWORKIN
31. **PLANNING ETHICALLY**
    RESPONSIBLE RESEARCH
    by JOAN E. SIEBER
32. **APPLIED RESEARCH DESIGN**
    by TERRY E. HEDRICK,
    LEONARD BICKMAN, and DEBRA J. ROG
33. **DOING URBAN RESEARCH**
    by GREGORY D. ANDRANOVICH
    and GERRY RIPOSA
34. **APPLICATIONS OF CASE STUDY RESEARCH**
    by ROBERT K. YIN
35. **INTRODUCTION TO FACET THEORY**
    by SAMUEL SHYE and DOV ELIZUR
    with MICHAEL HOFFMAN
36. **GRAPHING DATA**
    by GARY T. HENRY
37. **RESEARCH METHODS IN SPECIAL EDUCATION**
    by DONNA M. MERTENS
    and JOHN A. McLAUGHLIN
38. **IMPROVING SURVEY QUESTIONS**
    by FLOYD J. FOWLER, Jr.
39. **DATA COLLECTION AND MANAGEMENT**
    by MAGDA STOUTHAMER-LOEBER
    and WELMOET BOK VAN KAMMEN
40. **MAIL SURVEYS**
    by THOMAS W. MANGIONE
41. **QUALITATIVE RESEARCH DESIGN**
    (Third Edition)
    by JOSEPH A. MAXWELL
42. **ANALYZING COSTS, PROCEDURES,**
    PROCESSES, AND OUTCOMES
    IN HUMAN SERVICES
    by BRIAN T. YATES
43. **DOING LEGAL RESEARCH**
    by ROBERT A. MORRIS, BRUCE D. SALES,
    and DANIEL W. SHUMAN
44. **RANDOMIZED EXPERIMENTS FOR PLANNING**
    AND EVALUATION
    by ROBERT F. BORUCH
45. **MEASURING COMMUNITY INDICATORS**
    by PAUL J. GRUENEWALD, ANDREW J. TRENO,
    GAIL TAFF, and MICHAEL KLITZNER
46. **MIXED METHODOLOGY**
    by ABBAS TASHAKKORI and CHARLES TEDDLIE
47. **NARRATIVE RESEARCH**
    by AMIA LIEBLICH, RIVKA TUVAL-MASHIACH, and
    TAMAR ZILBER
48. **COMMUNICATING SOCIAL SCIENCE RESEARCH**
    TO POLICY-MAKERS
    by ROGER VAUGHAN and TERRY F. BUSS
49. **PRACTICAL META-ANALYSIS**
    by MARK W. LIPSEY and DAVID B. WILSON
50. **CONCEPT MAPPING FOR PLANNING**
    AND EVALUATION
    by MARY KANE and WILLIAM M. K. TROCHIM
51. **CONFIGURATIONAL COMPARATIVE METHODS**
    by BENOÎT RIHOUX and CHARLES C. RAGIN

SECOND EDITION

Methods for Policy Research

Taking Socially Responsible Action

Ann Majchrzak
University of Southern California

M. Lynne Markus
Bentley University

3 APPLIED SOCIAL RESEARCH METHODS SERIES

Los Angeles | London | New Delhi
Singapore | Washington DC

Los Angeles | London | New Delhi
Singapore | Washington DC

FOR INFORMATION:

SAGE Publications, Inc.
2455 Teller Road
Thousand Oaks, California 91320
E-mail: order@sagepub.com

SAGE Publications Ltd.
1 Oliver's Yard
55 City Road
London EC1Y 1SP
United Kingdom

SAGE Publications India Pvt. Ltd.
B 1/I 1 Mohan Cooperative Industrial Area
Mathura Road, New Delhi 110 044
India

SAGE Publications Asia-Pacific Pte. Ltd.
3 Church Street
#10-04 Samsung Hub
Singapore 049483

Acquisitions Editor: Helen Salmon
Assistant Editor: Kalie Koscielak
Editorial Assistant: Kaitlin Perry
Permissions Editor: Adele Hutchinson
Marketing Manager: Nicole Elliott
Project Editor: Veronica Stapleton Hooper
Copy Editor: Pam Schroeder
Typesetter: C&M Digitals (P) Ltd.
Proofreader: Sarah J. Duffy
Indexer: Molly Hall
Cover Designer: Candice Harman

Copyright © 2014 by SAGE Publications, Inc.

Printed in the United States of America

Library of Congress Cataloging-in-Publication Data

Majchrzak, Ann.

Methods for policy research: taking socially responsible action / Ann Majchrzak, M. Lynne Markus.—2nd Edition.

pages cm
Includes bibliographical references and index.

ISBN 978-1-4129-9780-5 (pbk.)

1. Policy sciences—Research. I. Markus, M. Lynne. II. Title.

H97.M35 2013
320.6072—dc23   2013005292

This book is printed on acid-free paper.

MIX
Paper from
responsible sources

FSC
www.fsc.org   FSC® C014174

14 15 16 17 10 9 8 7 6 5 4 3 2

Contents

Foreword to the First Edition   vii

Preface   ix

Acknowledgments   xi

About the Authors   xiii

Chapter 1: Make a Difference With Policy Research   1

Chapter 2: Launch the Policy Research Process   15

Chapter 3: Synthesize Existing Evidence   41

Chapter 4: Obtain New Evidence   63

Chapter 5: Design Policy Recommendations   93

Chapter 6: Expand Stakeholder Engagement   117

Chapter 7: Reflect on the Policy Research Voyage   137

References   149

Index   153

Foreword to the First Edition

The issue is a very old one indeed. How to bring knowledge to bear on policy decisions? Plato reflected upon it in the terms of his age. His ingenious solution was to unify in one person both analysis and policy making by crowning a philosopher king. If this solution was practical for a city-polity, I leave it to historians. It will not serve a complex modern society, in which knowledge is mass produced—and policy makers are never knowledge makers, even if this was their specialty before they were elected or appointed to their august offices.

Once one recognizes that two social positions—two specialties, two elites—at work are complementary but not reducible, all the issues Ann Majchrzak deals with (following very much on her own, work we started together) must be faced.

One problem might be called "blue yondering," the danger that the knowledge makers will build knowledge of interest and value to them. (Some campus-based researchers talk about "Robin Hooding" applied funds to advance their basic research.) A parallel problem is that of policy makers who heed not knowledge directly available to them, relevant to their decisions.

Assuming relevant knowledge and an open-minded policy maker, the problems of bridge design arise. In what form is knowledge best transmitted from the knowledge makers to the policy makers? Hefty tomes? Single-spaced, footnoted reprints? Or oral briefing, followed by "eyes-only" memos? (At least one president refused memos longer than one page, and another often asked information to be put on tape, for his TV set.)

Least understood—and Ann Majchrzak deserves much credit for stressing this point—is the role of power in the interaction between knowledge makers and policy makers. The same report will have much more of an impact—and in a way ought to—if submitted by a commission which built a wide coalition and consensus on its behalf (e.g., the Social Security Commission) than if submitted merely by a panel of experts. Ideas and data do *not* fly on their own wings. This does not mean that they have no role of their own: Naked power may be as weak as knowledge with backers. The combination works best to bridge knowledge and decision.

In the years to come, resources in both the public and the private sector will continue to be much in demand—that is, scarce. Hence, the commanding need to use them wisely. If Ann Majchrzak's book will get the audience it deserves, there is a fair chance we all will be richer for it.

—**Amitai Etzioni**
The George Washington University

Preface

This is a book about responsible and evidence-based decision making. It describes how to define policy research questions so that evidence can be applied to them, how to find and synthesize existing evidence, how to generate new evidence if needed, how to make acceptable recommendations that can solve policy problems without negative side effects, and how to describe evidence and recommendations in a manner that changes minds. This book is for the community of learners interested in improving decisions that affect people's lives. Policies are not just the decisions made by a country's rulers or elected officials; policies are also set by corporate executives, managers of department stores, and project leaders in nonprofit organizations pursuing environmental protection. In this book, we derive our suggestions from the fundamental belief that evidence-based decision making is superior to decisions based purely on opinion, intuition, and emotion. If we can convince one reader to consider the evidence systematically and responsibly before making a decision, and if we can help one individual to communicate evidence and recommendations in a way that facilitates real change, then this book has achieved the goals we set for ourselves when we sat down to write it.

This is a substantially different book than the first edition Ann Majchrzak wrote in 1984. It's a different book because the examples are updated. It's a different book because a lot has happened in society since 1984. It's also a different book because M. Lynne Markus joined Ann as a coauthor. Together, Ann and Lynne made the following improvements in this new edition:

1. Each chapter now has clearly defined activities, deliverables, and criteria for tracking successful performance of the activities, along with work-flow diagrams, and is tied together by artwork with a nautical theme depicting each chapter's phase in the policy research voyage.

2. Frameworks like the Policy Change Wheel and social, technical, organizational, regulatory, and market (STORM) context conditions make it easier for readers to remember what needs to be done.

3. New chapters were added on synthesizing available evidence (Chapter 3) and reflecting on policy research experiences (Chapter 7).

4. Examples have been updated and drawn from a variety of contexts, including international and business policy in addition to domestic issues.

5. Chapter 1: Make a Difference With Policy Research was substantially revised to reflect an action-orientation approach toward not just doing policy research but

also fostering change and emphasizing the importance of doing policy research responsibly.

6. Chapter 2: Launch the Policy Research Process was substantially revised to incorporate the new frameworks.

7. Chapter 3: Synthesize Existing Evidence is all new.

8. Chapter 4: Obtain New Evidence was updated to reflect the availability of web-based data for use in policy research.

9. Chapter 5: Design Policy Recommendations was substantially revised to emphasize the need for creativity as well as the use of frameworks in designing and evaluating recommendations.

10. Chapter 6: Expand Stakeholder Engagement was substantially revised to discuss how stakeholders need to become engaged in improving the Case for Change.

11. Chapter 7: Reflect on the Policy Research Voyage is all new.

We hope you enjoy the book, and we look forward to learning how you've made a difference with policy research. Bon voyage!

Acknowledgments

Many people helped us write this second edition of *Methods for Policy Research*. First, we were so inspired by the tenacity of the readership to the first edition of the book. Although the first edition was published in 1984, it continued to be purchased by sufficient numbers of readers to never be out of print despite the passage of time. This convinced us that interest in having a book that helps navigate the murky waters of policy research remains as strong today as it was almost 30 years ago!

Second, we would like to thank Elizabeth ("Lizzie") Kubo Kirschenbaum. When we started revising this book, we turned to Lizzie, a second-year undergraduate student at the Elliott School of International Relations, Honors Program, George Washington University, for administrative support. Quickly, though, we realized that she represented the audience for this book—the generation of students who care a great deal about the world around them and want to make a difference. So she became much more than our support person; she became our audience, helping us ensure that examples and exercises made sense to her and her peers. Lizzie also did the invaluable service of putting us in touch with Samantha ("Sammy") McBride, another amazingly bright undergraduate. Sammy did all the cartoon illustrations in this book. All we did was send to Sammy some general images and the text for the chapter, and she made one great illustration after another. Sammy has a career ahead of her as a graphics artist par excellence!

We would also like to thank other young people in our lives who have spurred us on to care about how to improve policy decision making. For Ann, those two people are her children, Jared and Becky Niemiec. Now that they are grown and out of the house, they particularly inspire me to see the world for not just what is wrong with it but what is right about it and how individuals can make a difference. Watching Jared at the age of 25 helping to make legislative changes that allow large container truck companies to add parts that make them more fuel efficient was inspirational to say the least! Watching Becky travel around the country, educating middle school children and tirelessly fighting for environmental protection inspired me to work harder to find ways to make the policy research process more doable for all.

Young people may create the future for us all, but there have been many "older" people who have been wise beyond their years to help us understand how to help others with this murky policy research process. We have been fortunate to work with corporate and government policy makers who have been willing to show us how they do it and what kind of help they really need from policy researchers. We've had the "opportunity" to fail in our own policy research efforts and then try again based on a new understanding of the policy research process. We have even had the opportunity of influencing a decision or two, giving us the optimism and enthusiasm that drove us to prepare this second edition.

We would like to thank the staff at Sage for encouraging us to prepare this new edition, for identifying reviewers that would be appropriate for this book, and for helping us focus our revisions. The reviewers were truly outstanding in challenging and directing us. As we were working through their comments, we didn't know who they were. Sage kindly unveiled their names to us upon preparing these acknowledgments, and we would like to thank them by name: Mary Fran T. Malone, University of New Hampshire; Lisa A. Baglione, Saint Joseph's University; Sherry Lowrance, The University of Georgia; Robert Bickel, Marshall University; Melissa Gross, The Florida State University; Kevin P. Donnelly, Bridgewater State College; Tony Payan, The University of Texas at El Paso; Andrew I. E. Ewoh, Kennesaw State University; Rebecca Nesbit, The University of North Carolina at Charlotte; Lawrence M. Mead, New York University; Haco Huang, California Lutheran University; Adam J. Newmark, Appalachian State University; Matthew Jones, Portland State University; Heather Kanenberg, Elizabethtown College; Meg Streams, Tennessee State University; and Juan D. Rogers, School of Public Policy, Georgia Institute of Technology.

Finally, personal friends and family have provided us the support we needed when we needed it. Amitai Etzioni, considered by us as one of the most important influences on policy research of the modern world, made the first edition possible. Peter Niemiec, Ann's husband, has been the most supportive husband an author could ever hope to have. Lynne wishes to thank her family, friends, and students and to acknowledge her debts to Peter F. Drucker, Paul Gray, and Rob Kling.

About the Authors

Ann Majchrzak (PhD, Social Psychology, University of California Los Angeles, 1980) is a professor of information and operations management at the Marshall School of Business, University of Southern California. She has been doing policy research since 1980 for U.S. government agencies, large and small nonprofits, and corporations. She also does research in her specific discipline of organizational and technological innovation, including studies on knowledge sharing, innovation, distributed cognition, emergent groups, virtual collaboration, collaboration in high-secure, volatile environments, emergency response, and innovation challenges. Her publications include books such as *The Human Side of Factory Automation* (Sage); articles in journals such as *Organization Science, Information Systems Research, IEEE Transactions on Engineering Management, Management Science, MIS Quarterly, Harvard Business Review,* and *Sloan Management Review;* and numerous book chapters and presentations to industry, government, and academics. She has served on three National Academy of Sciences Committees, is a Fellow of the Association for Information Systems, and is a senior editor for *Organization Science* and *MIS Quarterly.* For more information, see www.marshall.usc.edu/faculty/directory/majchrza.

M. Lynne Markus (PhD, Organizational Behavior, Case Western Reserve University, 1979) is The John W. Poduska, Sr. Professor of Information and Process Management at the Bentley University and a research affiliate at the Massachusetts Institute of Technology Sloan's Center for Information Systems Research. She does practice-oriented research for businesses, associations, nonprofits, and governments. Her specific areas of academic and practice-oriented research include the effective design, implementation, and use of information systems within and across organizations; the risks and unintended consequences of information technology use; and innovations in the governance and management of information technology. She has received several research grants from the U.S. National Science Foundation and recently summarized her research on the role of information technology in the mortgage crisis at a Securities and Exchange Commission roundtable. Her publications include several books and more than 100 articles in journals such as *MIS Quarterly, Information Systems Research,* and *Organization Science.* She served as a senior editor for *MIS Quarterly.* She was named a Fellow of the Association for Information Systems in 2004. In 2008, she won the Association for Information Systems Leo Award for Exceptional Lifetime Achievement in Information Systems. For more information, see https://faculty.bentley.edu/details.asp?uname=mlmarkus.

1

Make a Difference With Policy Research

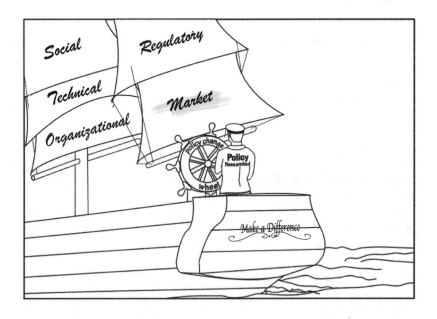

We wrote this book for people who want to change the world—or at least some part of it. You may want to make a difference in problems of truly global proportions, such as climate change, war, disease, famine, economic crisis, or water pollution. You may want to address problems that affect an entire country, such as persistent unemployment, racial and gender inequality and intolerance, worsening educational opportunities, or obesity. You may want to deal with issues that are more local in scope, such as inefficient and ineffective service delivery in your agency, poor profitability in your business, homelessness in your city, or deterioration in your neighborhood. Policy research can help you change the world responsibly.

We think of policy research as both a voyage and a destination. In this how-to book, we take you through the policy research voyage phase by phase. But it's important not to lose sight of the destination: *policy makers and*

implementers informed and motivated to act by your persuasive recommenda-
tions based on evidence-based, meaningful, and responsible policy research.

In this introductory chapter, we first answer some frequently asked questions about what policy research is, who does policy research, and what it
means to do policy research responsibly. Then, we describe the context in
which policy research happens and what this means for policy researchers.
Finally, we lay out the plan of the book.

FREQUENTLY ASKED QUESTIONS

Questions frequently asked about policy research include what it is, who does
it (or who can do it), and what it means to do policy research well, that is,
responsibly.

What Is Policy Research?

The term *policy research* refers both to a skillful process and to an outcome.
The process is a set of activities to perform and outputs to produce. The outcome is documented knowledge about a problem and about ways to solve the
problem combined with carefully reasoned recommendations for action.
Policy research involves using evidence to understand the causes and consequences of problems and the advantages, disadvantages, and risks of different
ways of dealing with problems. Evidence can include data already assembled
by others and new evidence collected especially for policy research purposes.
Evidence means facts, data, and experience—as opposed to assumptions,
theories, opinions, and values. But, of course, assumptions, theories, opinions,
and values—we call them *meaning*—are ever-present and affect both the
production of evidence and its interpretation and use. So policy research
involves working with both evidence and meaning to create outcomes that
help to change the world.

Policy research is not the only way to change the world. It is not the most-
used way. And it may not even be the best way in all circumstances. There are
other ways to change the world. You can change the world by leading and
participating in social, religious, political, or artistic movements. You can
change the world by leading and participating in organizations, governments,
and businesses. You can change the world by inventing new things and ideas.
You can change the world by educating, parenting, and helping. You can
change the world just by being who you are.

All these different ways of changing the world require people to take
actions, observe the consequences of those actions, and then change their

actions based on feedback. In some contexts, this is called *learning by doing*. In other contexts, this action–feedback–reaction cycle as applied to problem solving is called *entrepreneurship*—either social entrepreneurship (Bornstein & Davis, 2010) or business entrepreneurship (Drucker, 1985; Mullins & Komisar, 2009). Policy research can help this action–feedback–reaction cycle. Policy research is a process that attempts to support and persuade actors by providing them with well-reasoned, evidence-based, and responsible recommendations for decision making and action. So, even if you are changing the world in your own way, you can use policy research in your decisions to act. Whether you are a political leader, governmental official, or business manager, policy research can help.

Who Does Policy Research?

Policy researchers can be found all over the place. Some policy researchers are professionals. Often called policy analysts, some professional policy researchers are employed in government agencies, nongovernmental organizations (NGOs, like foundations and charities), and think tanks. They conduct analyses (often using economic methods such as cost-benefit analysis) of policy areas such as employment, education, health care, and housing. Professional policy researchers may be academics in universities concerned with policy questions related to their areas of expertise, whether that be social work, criminal justice, or real estate. Some professional policy researchers are not called policy researchers at all; they are called business strategists, financial analysts, or management consultants who use economic and social science methods to systematically evaluate the costs, benefits, and risks of investments; of innovations like new products, services, or processes; and of new organizational designs and management systems. No matter what the job title, professional policy researchers typically study proposed improvement opportunities or solutions to problems—we call them *interventions*. These interventions may be identified by policy makers, executives, and funding agencies for study or may be derived by the policy researcher's evidence gathering. The product of the policy researcher's research, documented in reports and papers, is a set of persuasive and evidence-based recommendations to policy makers, executives, or funding agencies about the decisions or actions that should be taken.

Policy research isn't just for professionals. It is also a useful skill and resource for people who do not do policy research full time or for pay. Almost anyone can be an "amateur" policy researcher: a teacher, social worker, manager, staff member, parent, athlete, or citizen who is troubled by some state of affairs, passionate about change, and motivated enough to systematically

explore what is known and not known about a problem's causes, consequences, and solutions. Amateur—we might even say *accidental*—policy
researchers differ from professionals in at least three ways.

First, accidental policy researchers, unlike professionals, may not have a
client at the outset of their policy research journey. That is, they may not have
someone who expects to receive their reports and recommendations. Accidental
policy researchers typically study policy problems and interventions solely
because of their interest or concern. Accidental policy researchers are often
motivated to address the problems of a particular vulnerable or victimized
group such as acquired immune deficiency syndrome (AIDS) sufferers, people
who were laid off in a financial crisis, poor children not well served by their
schools, homeless people, and so on. Victimized groups are potential benefi-
ciaries of policy research, but they are not usually its clients. Clients are those
who can take action based on policy research recommendations. Therefore,
accidental policy researchers may have to find clients for their research.
Professionals, on the other hand, know who their clients are—the people or
organizations that commissioned their research.

A second difference from professional policy researchers is that accidental
policy researchers often have more options about what they do after arriving
at a recommendation for action. Professional policy researchers often do only
policy research. When they finish one project, they go on the next policy
research project. Accidental policy researchers can do that, too. Or they can
move into an advocacy role, devoting their energies to mobilizing others to
take action now that they have a persuasive case for change. Or accidental
policy researchers can move into an entrepreneurial role, deciding to try to
implement their own recommendations. They might do this through a start-up
organization, whether a nonprofit, a for-profit, or a benefit corporation. For
example, if an accidental policy researcher came up with an idea for a new
product or service that would help a victimized group, he or she might set up
a new organization to market the product or service. Accidental policy
researchers might also become entrepreneurs inside the organization in which
they work. This is sometimes called *intrapreneurship.* If, for example, Susan
is an accidental policy researcher persuasively recommending a better process
for service delivery in her organization, she may become an intrapreneur,
implementing the intervention herself.

A third difference from professional policy researchers is that accidental
policy researchers often have more flexibility in the methods they can use to
do their policy research, including using primary research methods such as
interviews, field experiments, surveys, and case studies. In contrast, professional policy researchers are often expected—and limited—to use a policy
research approach referred to as *secondary analysis,* that is, quantitative

analyses using sophisticated statistical procedures and economic models of large data archives of facts about employment, health, economic activity, and so forth. Professional policy researchers are sometimes also expected to conduct cost-benefit analyses of alternative interventions. Accidental policy researchers are not restricted in this fashion.

This book provides guidance for accidental as well as professional policy researchers. The policy research process as described in this book is not formulaic; it demands creativity. At the same time, it is systematic, such that it is disciplined, rigorous, and in a word, professional. We believe that a professional approach to policy research is just as appropriate for amateurs as it is for professionals. Even if you are the ultimate client for your own policy research, doing policy research as professionally as you can within your resources of time, money, and other people's help is the *responsible* thing to do.

What Does It Mean to Do Policy Research Responsibly?

Responsible? What do we mean by that word? We mean being sensitive to the potential harm you can do to people and the environment by even the best-intentioned interventions. The reason to do high-quality policy research, even if no one is paying you to do it, is that it will help you avoid recommending or implementing a cure that is worse than the disease.

History is full of stories about negative consequences—not just of accidents or natural events like earthquakes and volcanic eruptions but also of actions and nonactions (decisions to do nothing) that people may have deliberately taken for what they thought were good reasons. Think of the atom bomb dropped on Hiroshima, failure to delay the launch of the Challenger space shuttle, the policy of apartheid in South Africa, or the recurrent noninvestments in levee repair in New Orleans prior to Hurricane Katrina. When negative consequences happen, we may assume that people acted with bad motives or that they were powerless to act differently, when in fact, some people acted (or didn't act) deliberately but without considering the possible negative consequences as well as they could have done.

We believe that many policy changes have negative consequences, sometimes worse than the problems they are meant to solve, even when the changes are made with the best of intentions. At the same time, we believe that many of these negative consequences can be anticipated and therefore avoided or mitigated in advance (rather than just coped with after the fact). Anticipating negative consequences requires (1) knowledge of evidence—what worked and didn't work in the past, (2) disciplined imagination about the future, and (3) the experience-tested methods of policy research we present in this book.

Although doing good policy research cannot eliminate all possibility of negative consequences, we believe that good policy research is a must for anyone who wants to change the world responsibly.

THE CONTEXT OF POLICY RESEARCH AND IMPLICATIONS FOR POLICY RESEARCHERS

One of the experience-tested tools of policy research that we discuss in this book is the *theory of the problem*—a theory of why a policy problem exists and how it produces problematic outcomes. (To solve the problem, you will also need a *theory of the intervention*—when, why, and how it works.) We briefly describe our theory of how policy change happens, where policy research fits in, and what this theory means for policy research and researchers.

The Context of Policy Research

One widely held theory of how policy change happens (or should happen—it is not always easy to know whether some theories are descriptive of what actually happens or prescriptive of what should happen) is the rational choice model (Munger, 2000; Sabatier, 2007; Stone, 2012). Rational choice theory holds that policy makers base their decisions and actions on a systematic analysis of costs, benefits, and risks of alternative courses of action. Rational choice theory does not necessarily assume that policy makers are omniscient. The theory acknowledges all sorts of limits on rational decision making—such as time constraints, imperfect information, and cognitive biases. As a result, rational choice theory does not rule out the possibility of bad decisions and unintended consequences.

We don't subscribe to the rational choice theory of the policy process. We believe that social and business policy change happens through contests of values and ideas (Stone, 2012). Even if policy makers had perfect information about the consequences of proposed actions, there would almost never be complete consensus in an organization, let alone society, that a recommended action is the right thing to do. Because conflicts about evidence and meaning are inevitable in policy situations of any scope or importance, the chances are great that whatever policy change occurs, if any, will be a synthesis or resolution of various conflicting proposals. Sometimes, the synthesis will be a compromise that disappoints everyone. Sometimes, it will have truly horrible outcomes. Sometimes, it will be the best possible solution. The goal of responsible policy research is to try to change the consensus of opinion leaders toward the best possible solution given circumstances and current knowledge while recognizing that knowledge is imperfect and the label *best possible* always implies making value judgments.

A Hypothetical Example of Policy Research in Action

Let's suppose a policy researcher working for a consumer products company was asked to evaluate an investment in a new manufacturing facility. Let's assume that the researcher conducted a systematic analysis of business conditions and possible alternative future outcomes depending on whether the new facility was built or not. During the policy research process, the policy researcher gathered evidence and meaning by talking to stakeholder groups, including workers, managers, citizens, government officials, and representatives at other companies.

With the policy research in hand, the policy researcher might then be confident that the new facility would enable the company to grow rapidly, to expand its workforce considerably, to return more profits to shareholders, and to yield more tax revenues for the nearby town. At the same time, the researcher would also be aware that the new facility was planned for a different state than where the existing facility operated. The researcher would also know that the old facility would be closed down and all its workers and managers laid off and that the company's two main suppliers would also end up closing their facilities as well, further harming employment in the town.

After examining all the evidence, the policy researcher would then make several alternative recommendations to executives, one of which is a creative recommendation that protects the current employees and the town where the old facility was located. (Here's an assignment for you! Can you give an example of a recommendation that protects current employees and the town?)

Executive policy makers in the company will then decide which recommendation to implement. They may decide to implement one of the policy researchers' creative alternatives. However, they may completely ignore the policy researcher's creative recommendations and simply close the existing plant despite the harmful consequences to the town. Finally, they may decide to take no action at all and keep the existing plant running for a while longer, leaving the policy researcher aware of the possibility of an impending plant closure but not able to share that possibility with any of those in the town.

Three points should be clear from this hypothetical example of policy research. First, the policy researcher is not the one who makes the final decision or takes the action (unless the policy researcher shifts out the research role into an entrepreneurial role). As a result, what actually happens may not reflect the policy researcher's analysis or recommendations. Actual policy change is rarely if ever a straightforward product of rational analysis and choice. Instead, it is often a complex compromise resulting from conflicts over ideas and values.

Second, even if policy research does not influence the decision makers in the short run, it may change the course of events in time. In the short term, a single policy research study may not change policy makers' minds. However, over time, the results of many policy studies can accumulate and become decisive in persuading policy makers to act in ways that a policy researcher recommends.

A third lesson of our hypothetical example is that the policy researcher has a responsibility to make, if not the best possible recommendations, at least very good ones that are rigorously grounded in the evidence. Making good recommendations can be extremely challenging because recommendations always involve questions of meaning and value judgments as well as analyses of evidence. Significant creativity is often required to identify ways to navigate value conflicts among different stakeholder groups (e.g., shareholders, workers and management, citizens, the planet).

If a seemingly straightforward business decision such as investing in a new manufacturing facility can raise so many issues, it should be no surprise that policy research conducted to solve public policy issues is even more challenging, and rational choice theory is even less likely to apply. Like many others (Munger, 2000; Sabatier, 2007; Stone, 2012), we see policy change as occurring in a turbulent environment. That environment is turbulent in part because it includes many stakeholder groups with different needs, values, and concerns. Among the stakeholders of public policy issues are people afflicted by social and economic problems, people who may be affected (positively or negatively) by solutions to the problem (e.g., care givers and service providers, large corporations, citizens, taxpayers) and policy makers and policy researchers who have to think about how their policy recommendations may affect their own careers and livelihoods. In addition, the environment in which policy change occurs is turbulent because of conflicts over theories, evidence, and values. In this stormy environment, solutions to policy problems are often incremental, even when major change is needed.

In the turbulent environment of policy change, policy research can sometimes make a difference. But it's important to recognize that policy research can sometimes make a difference for the worse. This can happen when policy researchers behave irresponsibly, for instance, by biasing their recommendations: selecting or distorting the evidence to support their own values and preferred solutions. The recommendations of irresponsible policy research are sometimes accepted and implemented. When that happens, the outcomes are grim: The problem is not solved, the problem actually gets worse, or the side effects of the solution are worse than the problem.

Sadly, even responsible policy research can sometimes also make a difference for the worse when partisans of opposing views discredit the research or distort its findings to support opposite conclusions. When this happens, good interventions for complex problems may become politically unacceptable. Doing policy research as professionally as possible can help, but it cannot eliminate the possibility of this negative outcome. Responsible policy researchers must constantly remain aware of the stormy context of policy research. Like every other action in life, policy research can have unintended consequences.

Implications for Policy Researchers

Here is the paradox you face as a policy researcher. On the one hand, policy change is more turbulent and less predictable than a rational choice theory of policy change. Yet, on the other hand, systematic policy research that makes use of evidence (as well as meaning) is needed to make recommendations that have some possibility of being accepted, despite the fact that policy makers do not always take the decisions and actions that policy researchers recommend.

What this paradox means for you is that policy research has limitations. You will encounter flimsy evidence, difficulties in obtaining new evidence, challenges of balancing evidence and meaning, and an extreme difficulty of changing closed minds. But unless you provide decision makers with evidence about the possible effects of different kinds of interventions for a problem, you are leaving decision makers with nothing more for guidance than common sense, opinion, and demagoguery. *We know that it takes passion to change the world, but it takes more than passion to make the world a better place.* It takes critical thinking, evidence, meaning, and careful value judgments.

Let us sum up, then, some of the key characteristics of good policy research. First, good policy research is (1) credible because it is informed by evidence and unbiased (to the extent possible) about the pros, cons, and risks of problems and potential interventions; (2) meaningful to, and engaging of, representatives of stakeholder groups, which include policy makers, people who suffer from problems, and people who may be affected by solutions; (3) responsible, by considering a broad spectrum of potential negative consequences of change; (4) creative, because your policy situation may need new or different solutions than those used elsewhere; and (5) manageable for policy researchers, that is, doable within the time and resources you have available.

Second, good policy research requires good policy research questions. Good questions do not define the problem in terms of one solution, as the following question does: "How can we improve citizens' access to guns for self-defense?" Good policy questions are broad enough to encourage a search for more and possibly better solutions. With more solution alternatives, there is a greater likelihood of finding one solution aligned with stakeholders' beliefs and values. Good policy research questions also do not rule out the possibility that some, maybe all, interventions may have worse effects than allowing the current situation to continue unchanged.

A third characteristic of good policy research is that it is creative. Creativity, particularly in the design of policy recommendations, is needed for many reasons. Evidence about the causes of problems may be missing, weak, conflicting, or contested. The same could be true of evidence about the costs, benefits, and risks of possible solutions. In addition, problems and solutions can mean different things to and for different stakeholders. That is, stakeholders rarely value the same things, and they are usually unequally affected by the problem or its solutions.

Creativity is required when designing good recommendations for another reason as well: There are so many different types of possible interventions from which to choose. Possible ways to solve problems include training and education, new processes and technologies, new organizational arrangements, taxes, laws, incentives, monitoring, punishments, and many more (Bardach, 2009). Effective intervention in a situation may need to target a point quite distant from where a problem is observed. For example, instead of recommending education for smokers, you may want to recommend restrictions on the marketing practices of tobacco companies.

Still another reason that creativity is required for good intervention design is that some problems can only be solved by interventions in multiple aspects of a problem at the same time. For instance, to improve children's learning at school, you may need also to improve support for their learning at home, their nutrition, and their access to health care.

A fourth characteristic of good policy research is that it requires having a detailed understanding of the context in which the problem exists and having a theory of how and why the problem occurs. We spoke of policy change as occurring in a turbulent or stormy context. In this book, we encourage you to examine all aspects of a problem's context for *malleable variables* (sometimes also called *change levers*) that can serve as good targets of intervention. Later in the book, we use the STORM acronym—referring to the social, technical, organizational, regulatory, and market conditions surrounding a problem—to help you broaden your search for malleable variables. Stakeholder analysis and the Policy Change Wheel are additional tools we provide later for helping you analyze the context and articulate your theories of problems and interventions.

A final characteristic of good policy research is that it rarely comes easily. It is hard work, it takes time, and it doesn't always win you friends. But it is important, meaningful, and fun work to do!

THE POLICY RESEARCH VOYAGE

We use the metaphor of a sea voyage to describe the policy research process. Figure 1.1 provides a map of the voyage. As in many real travels, the policy research process does not always follow a straight line, as the map might suggest. There are occasional side trips, and some activities are repeated again and again. (Reframing the policy research question has a lot in common with packing, unpacking, and repacking your bags when traveling!) We try to capture these iterations in the details of each chapter.

Each chapter describes the major activities you perform and the *deliverables,* that is, the outputs you produce at each stage of the voyage. In addition, the chapters discuss intermediate goals—we call them tracking indicators— that you can use to know whether you are staying on course throughout the iterations and inevitable obstacles that arise in any policy research voyage.

As you read through the next chapter, Chapter 2, you will see that it concerns the activities and deliverables involved in launching your policy research process. You start this Launch Phase with a policy research question that is as good as you can make it at the time, given what you know. A good policy research question is one that is broad enough to be meaningful but focused enough to be manageable given the time and resources you have available. As you familiarize yourself with the policy problem, you progressively refine the question, which helps to focus your subsequent research. Tools to help you refine the policy research question are presented in Chapter 2, including the Policy Change Wheel, STORM context conditions, and Stakeholder Analysis. Other important activities in the Launch Phase are to identify experts and other stakeholders who may be able to help you and to enlist some of them, formally or informally, as your advisers.

Chapter 3 outlines the goals, activities, and deliverables of the Synthesize Existing Evidence Phase of the policy research voyage. Here, starting with your more focused research question, you systematically collect, analyze, and synthesize evidence that already exists about the problem and possible interventions for improving the problem. We discuss good sources of evidence and ways to assess the strength of the evidence. By the end of this phase, you should have a very good idea about what is known about the problem or its solutions and, more important, about what is not known. This is important because you need to decide whether the existing evidence is

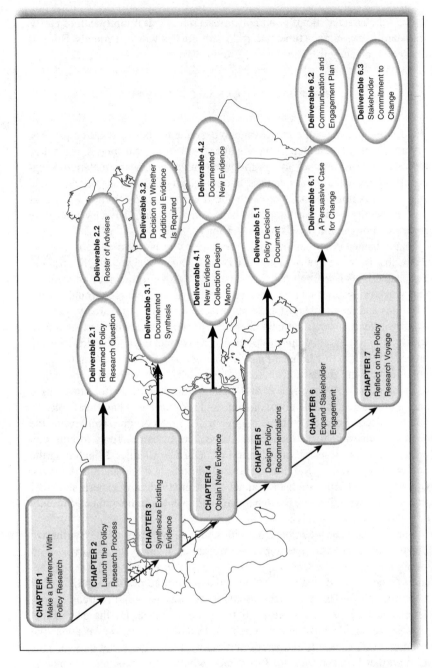

Figure 1.1 The Policy Research Voyage Map

CHAPTER 1
Make a Difference With
Policy Research

CHAPTER 2
Launch the Policy
Research Process

Deliverable 2.1
Reframed Policy
Research Question

Deliverable 2.2
Roster of Advisers

CHAPTER 3
Synthesize Existing
Evidence

Deliverable 3.1
Documented
Synthesis

Deliverable 3.2
Decision on Whether
Additional Evidence
Is Required

CHAPTER 4
Obtain New Evidence

Deliverable 4.1
New Evidence
Collection Design
Memo

Deliverable 4.2
Documented
New Evidence

CHAPTER 5
Design Policy
Recommendations

Deliverable 5.1
Policy Decision
Document

CHAPTER 6
Expand Stakeholder
Engagement

Deliverable 6.1
A Persuasive Case
for Change

Deliverable 6.2
Communication and
Engagement Plan

Deliverable 6.3
Stakeholder
Commitment to
Change

CHAPTER 7
Reflect on the Policy
Research Voyage

strong enough for you to make confident policy recommendations (as described Chapter 5) or whether you need to collect additional evidence (as discussed in Chapter 4).

Chapter 4 focuses on the Obtain New Evidence Phase of the policy research voyage. This phase starts with a policy research question about what is not known (about the problem or its solutions). Answering this question may involve *secondary analysis*—statistical studies of data published in archives. However, other primary data collection methods may be better for your focused research question, including interviewing, conducting surveys and case studies, and creating field experiments. Chapter 4 covers the basics of research design, ways to increase your confidence in the results, and how to obtain new evidence ethically.

You now have a wealth of existing and possibly also new evidence about the policy problem and its solutions. But your job is not done; you must extract from the evidence a set of action recommendations for policy makers. Doing this well is a challenging and creative design activity; we call the phase Design Policy Recommendations. A critical first step in this phase—the subject of Chapter 5—is to develop what we call the Base Case, a description of the current situation and its negative outcomes, against which each of several alternative solutions will be compared. We explain the importance of assessing each alternative fairly using the same evaluation criteria rather than attempting to stack the deck in favor of the alternative you think is best. Ultimately, you will combine information about the Base Case and about the alternative interventions into a brief, well-structured, and persuasive decision document that informs policy makers and encourages them to take action.

You are still not done yet, even after making your recommendations to policy makers! At this point, your recommendations have been based primarily on the evidence and have not yet fully been tested for meaningfulness, that is, aligned with stakeholders' assumptions, theories, opinions, and values. If your recommendations do not align well, they may not be adopted or they may be resisted; as a result, your recommendations will not improve the problem or will have unacceptable negative side effects. In the Expand Stakeholder Engagement Phase, outlined in Chapter 6, you seek to gain stakeholders' support for your recommendations through a persuasive Case for Change. Of course, during this phase, you may also decide that you have to modify your recommendations to make them more meaningful.

The last chapter, Chapter 7, presents our reflections on the Policy Research Voyage. We distill the advice of the previous chapters into a set of principles for doing meaningful and impactful policy research.

CONCLUSION

Methods for Policy Research is meant to be an inspirational book. By the time you finish reading, we hope you will know what good policy research is, know how it can help create positive social and organizational change, have the skills you need to do good policy research, and be inspired to do good policy research on problems that are meaningful to you, even if you don't do policy research as a profession. If, after reading this book, you do not have all the resources you need to do good policy research alone, the knowledge and skills you learn should still help you select good advisers and research partners. In addition, you should be able to help others in their policy research voyages.

There are many ways to change the world. Social and business entrepreneurs change the world by implementing change, that is, by intervening in the existing state of affairs. Policy makers (e.g., legislators, investors, donors) change the world by making decisions and by supplying entrepreneurs with needed resources (e.g., legislative mandate, funding) for success. Policy researchers can also change the world—by changing people's minds. Policy researchers can use the tools described in this book to inform policy makers, entrepreneurs, and people affected by problems and to encourage them to act in ways that are evidence based, meaningful, and responsible. By synthesizing what is known about problems and solutions, by obtaining new evidence about what is not known, by designing recommendations for action, and by engaging stake-holders, policy researchers can envision and stimulate optimism for creative new solutions that solve problems without creating worse ones. Policy researchers can make a difference. Bon voyage!

2

Launch the Policy Research Process

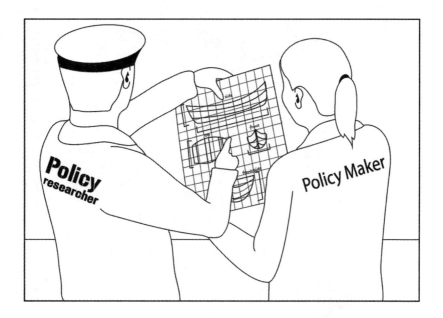

SUMMARY

This chapter explores the first phase of the policy research process: Launch. In this phase, you iteratively reframe the policy research question as you familiarize yourself with the policy problem. We provide you with frameworks to help direct and organize your knowledge gathering: the Policy Change Wheel, STORM context conditions, and Stakeholder Analysis. Additionally, in this process, you will identify a group of advisers willing to help you through the research. The activities and major deliverables of the Launch Phase are summarized in Figure 2.1. Prior to walking you through each of the six activities and two deliverables, it is important to explain your goal for the six activities and how you will be able to evaluate your performance of these activities. For this reason, we start this chapter, and all others,

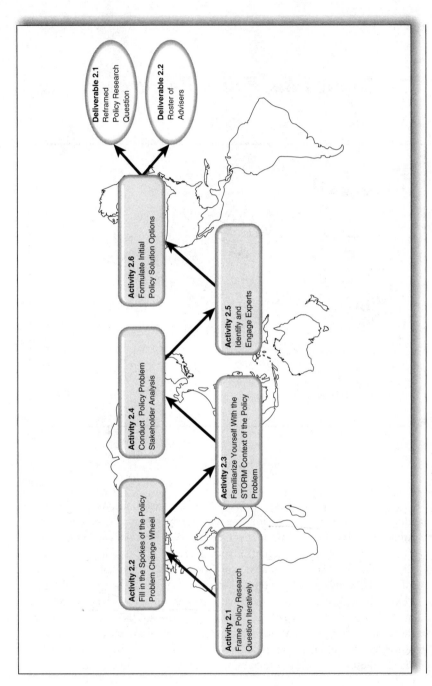

Figure 2.1 The Launch Phase Voyage Map

with not only this summary but also a discussion of indicators by which you can track your progress.

LAUNCH PHASE TRACKING INDICATORS

This section explains the two indicators you can use to help you know that you're doing a good job as you perform Launch Phase activities and produce Launch Phase deliverables. The criteria are

1. The M2 (Meaningfulness and Manageability) Test

2. Engaged Stakeholders

Tracking Indicator 2.1 Meaningfulness and Manageability

Policy research requires both meaningfulness and manageability. This is what we call the M2 test of policy research.

Meaningfulness means that, at the completion of your policy research process, your research makes a difference in the policy domain. That difference may be made by producing implementable recommendations likely to solve the policy problem. Or that difference may be made by resolving differences in assumptions between stakeholders about causes of the policy problem. Or the difference may be made by providing new evidence that helps to narrow the possible solution alternatives.

While anything you do might be meaningful to someone working in the policy domain, the meaningfulness of policy research derives from improving policy makers' understanding of the policy problem. If your research simply improves your own understanding (as you might do in purely academic research), it fails the M2 test. If your research simply tells policy makers what they already know, it fails the M2 test. Thus, as you launch your policy research process, it helps to keep in mind the policy makers whom you would like to help. These policy makers may be advocates in the policy making process, decision makers in your corporation, legislative staff members, regulatory officials, or others. The important point is that your policy research should provide them with increased understanding, enabling them to make better, more informed decisions. For example, legislative staff members often need information about the relative costs and benefits of different solution alternatives; informing them about a better way to implement one solution for one segment of the population in need may be less meaningful to them if that group is not part of the legislator's constituency.

Simply making your policy research meaningful is not enough. It must also be manageable for you. *Manageability* means that your policy research process consists of a set of activities that you can do with your own resources or resources you can muster. If your research plan is too extensive and takes too much time, you may lose your window of opportunity to influence decision makers. Or the policy problem may require resources you do not have: more technical knowledge, international access, or language skills. If you launch a policy research process so grand in scope that you can't accomplish it in the time available, you fail the M2 test. So you need to be concerned not just with meaningfulness of the policy research but whether the policy research is manageable by you.

There is a tension between meaningfulness and manageability. The more meaningful your policy research, the more issues you will need to consider, the more complex conditions you will have to examine, and the more elements that will need to be included in your policy research. Complexity, multiple conditions, and many elements make the policy research process less manageable because it takes more time and more resources. Manageability doesn't mean that you should focus your policy research question so narrowly that it is no longer meaningful. Nor does it mean launching a meaningful research effort that you cannot carry out. Never give one up for the other: Make your policy research question as meaningful as possible within the constraints of manageability. The activities in this chapter help you to develop a policy research question that meets the M2 test. And the M2 test is a good indicator that you are on track in the Launch Phase.

Tracking Indicator 2.2 Stakeholder Engagement

Policy research only succeeds with the help of stakeholders. As defined in Chapter 1, *stakeholders* are individuals and organizations that have a stake (i.e., a personal interest) in decisions made about the policy problem. Stakeholders include people who suffer from the problem (e.g., poor people without access to affordable health care), people who have resources to apply to the problem (e.g., medical insurance companies), people who make decisions about the problem (e.g., policy makers), and people who will be affected by interventions made to help solve the problem (e.g., doctors who have to use electronic medical records).

Because of their interests (stake) in the policy problem, engaged stakeholders can be very helpful to you in your policy research journey. They can provide information about the policy problem. They may be aware of the latest research on a policy problem or the current status of a proposal winding its way through the legislative branches of the government. More important, through their behaviors, networks, resources, attention, and enthusiasm, they can increase the implementability of your proposed solutions. For example, they may know donkey owners who can deliver medicines when buses fail; they may know who in the social hierarchy of an Indian reservation needs to be consulted when a change in Indian health services is under consideration.

To engage stakeholders so they share their information and resources with you, you must do far more than simply ask them questions. You need to develop relationships with them; you need to learn enough about them to become aware of needs that you might be able to fulfill as you work with them during your policy research. For example, if your stakeholders might benefit from meeting others facing similar problems, perhaps you can help them meet others during your research. Or if you discover that the burdens on the shoulders of your stakeholders are so acute that they could benefit from a sympathetic ear, you can help them by listening. Or if you determine that the stakeholders need data about the prevalence of their plight, you can help them by sharing the results of your study with them when it is done.

To know whether your stakeholders are engaged, observe their behavior. Do they volunteer information or advice that makes your policy research more meaningful and manageable? If so, then you have engaged stakeholders. Signs of disengaged stakeholders include stakeholders who are too busy to schedule time with you, not sharing information with you that you think they might have, never offering you advice, and arguing with you about the basic value of your research. So as you proceed through the Launch Phase, look for indicators of engaged or disengaged stakeholders.

LAUNCH PHASE ACTIVITIES

Now that you know the indicators to track while you move through the Launch Phase, it's time to learn the activities you will perform. There are six activities in the Launch Phase, as shown in Figure 2.1:

Activity 2.1: Frame Policy Research Question Iteratively

Activity 2.2: Fill in the Spokes of the Policy Problem Change Wheel

Activity 2.3: Familiarize Yourself With the STORM Context of the Policy Problem

Activity 2.4: Conduct Policy Problem Stakeholder Analysis

Activity 2.5: Identify and Engage Experts

Activity 2.6: Formulate Initial Policy Solution Options

We discuss each of these activities in turn.

Activity 2.1 Frame the Policy Research Question Iteratively

This is where you really start the policy research process: by starting to frame the policy research question and then iteratively getting more and more precise about the question so that it can be addressed by existing or new evidence. Sometimes, if you have a specific client, you will be tasked by the client decision maker—such as a legislator, government research funding agency, or your boss at work—to conduct a policy research study on a specific policy area, social problem, or business issue to generate recommendations. You may know a great deal about the topic already, or you may not. Sometimes, you will not only be informed about the specific policy area you are to study but by the policy research question you should address. The question may be very general, such as "What issues does global warming raise?" Or the question may be very specific, such as "What are the likely costs and benefits of improved seawalls for preventing shoreline erosion?" If you don't have a client, you will have an interest in a policy area and a question about that area, such as "How do I reduce emissions in my city?" This becomes your starting policy research question.

Whatever the question you start with, you need to progressively reframe the question to meet the M2 test. You will not be able to answer the question "How can global warming be reduced?" if you have only three days to come up with recommendations. But, in three days, you may be able to answer a related question reframed more narrowly: "How much effect would a particular cap on CO_2 emissions be likely to have on the rate of Antarctica's ice sheet melting if the cap was implemented today?"

To reframe the policy research question, we offer several guidelines that will eventually lead you to a policy research question that meets the M2 test. First, it's very useful to develop a personal connection to the problem. By personal connection, we mean a clear image of what may happen if trends continue as they are or a clear image of what will be accomplished if your policy research succeeds at convincing a policy maker to take action. For global warming research, this personal connection might be the image of a small child in the Marshall Islands living in fear of the next big storm that may wash away his or her town, the image of Easter Island artifacts floating away because of rising sea tides, or the image of a family in Louisiana unable to return home after a hurricane because their home has been flooded. When you can easily conjure up personal connection images about the policy problem, and these images make you want to act to change them, then your research is meaningful to you and will keep you motivated when barriers get in your way. If you don't have the personal connection images, keep reframing the question to be narrower and narrower so that you can get the image in your mind. Perhaps you have difficulty conjuring up images about global warming, but you can easily visualize a polar bear drowning in a sea without icebergs; so your question may need to be focused, for you, specifically on addressing iceberg dissipation.

Another guideline for policy research question reframing to meet the M2 test is to focus *either* on *causes* of the policy problem or *solutions* to the policy problem, but not both at the same time. For global warming research, for example, "What are the reasons for global warming?" and "What are solutions to global warming?" are both good policy research questions. But trying to include both questions in the same policy research study will make the study less manageable; picking one at a time is usually better.

Another M2 guideline is that the question should not define a specific solution into the policy problem (Bardach, 2009). For example, the question "How do we increase the number of shelters so that the number of homeless families can be reduced?" assumes that shelters reduce homelessness. This assumption fails the meaningful aspect of the M2 test because shelters are unlikely alone to reduce homelessness. The question will need to be reframed either as a question specifically about the value of shelters for homelessness or as a question about the ways in which shelters, in connection with other interventions, may help reduce homelessness.

A final guideline for passing the M2 test is to reframe the question to focus on issues for which evidence is needed. During the Launch Phase, you will get a general idea of what is already known about a problem or its solution. You may find, for example, that other people have already answered the question "Does the Head Start Program increase children's readiness to learn when they enter first grade?" It might be a waste of your time and effort to devote more research to that question. Instead, your research might be more meaningful to policy makers if you reframed the question as "Does children's participation in the Head Start Program improve their career success later in life?"

Activity 2.2 Fill in the Spokes of the Policy Problem Change Wheel

To familiarize yourself with a new policy problem, we offer you a framework to help you know where to start, how to prioritize your knowledge-seeking time, and how to organize the information you collect. We call the framework the *Policy Problem Change Wheel.*

The Policy Problem Change Wheel, shown in Figure 2.2, asks you a set of short W questions about the policy problem; your job is to learn whether there are already answers to each question and what those answers are. The Wheel helps you think about the policy area comprehensively, which in turn will stimulate your creative juices. The Wheel is helpful in analyzing both policy problems and policy solutions; we refer to it repeatedly throughout the book. You can use the Policy Problem Change Wheel early in the Launch Phase to learn what is already known about different aspects of the problem, which will help you reframe your research question on what is not already known. Later in the Launch Phase (Activity 2.6), you can develop a Policy Solution Change Wheel, in which case the W questions focus on the solutions you will evaluate. But for now, you will use the Wheel to focus on the problem. Below, we describe each spoke in the Wheel.

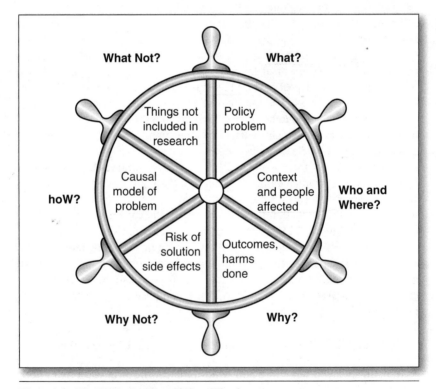

Figure 2.2 The Policy Problem Change Wheel

What? The "What?" question in the Wheel refers to the situation you hope to improve or the problem you hope to solve. The situation may range from increasing revenue at a firm to eliminating gender inequality in the workplace, global poverty, or AIDS.

What Not? The "What Not?" question helps you narrow the scope of your research question by excluding certain aspects of the problem. This is important both for manageability and to avoid falling into the expectations management trap. In this trap, the people for whom you are doing policy research reject your conclusions because you didn't study what they expected you to study. By making the "What Not?" clear, you can avoid the expectations trap. An example of using "What Not?" to reframe a policy research question of "What can be done to reduce the CO_2 emissions that contribute to global warming?" is to reframe the question to be "What can be done to reduce CO_2 emissions from nonanimal sources?" The reframed question excludes a focus on animal methane as a possible contributor to global warming.

Who and Where? "Who and Where?" refers to the context of the problem in your policy research question. We describe context in more detail in Activity 2.3: Familiarize Yourself With the STORM Context of the Policy Problem. Understanding the context of the problem is important for two reasons. First, it helps clarify the scope of your question. If you're interested in finding ways to reduce health care costs in the United States, the "Who and Where?" is the United States. By specifying the United States as your "Who and Where?," you make it clear to your audience that you're not trying to solve the problem of health care costs in The Netherlands. In addition, specifying the "Who and Where?" keeps you aware that information about how the problem was solved in The Netherlands may not be entirely relevant to solving the problem in the United States. A second reason for specifying the context is that it helps you to think about what effect the context may have on the problem. For example, if you are interested in reducing the spread of disease, you need to understand that conditions promoting the spread of disease are different in Appalachia than in urban ghettos.

hoW? The "hoW?" question of the Wheel refers to your theory, or *causal model,* of how the policy problem occurs. We often draw the theory of the problem as a causal diagram because it aids in communication with policy makers. In a causal model, the antecedent conditions or underlying causes of the problem are shown on the left, the consequences or symptoms of the problem are shown on the right, and in the middle are the mechanisms or pathways by which initial conditions are turned into problems. For example, you may theorize that the conditions leading to global warming (left side of the causal model) are coal-burning power plants, gas-powered transport vehicles, and animal methane emissions. On the right side of the causal model are the outcomes, such as higher average water and land temperatures, increased severity of weather, increased rates of sea ice melting, rises in sea level, and species extinction. In the middle of the causal model, you would place mechanisms that convert initial conditions into problematic outcomes: high CO_2 emissions and atmospheric layers that trap the emissions.

The "hoW?" causal model depicts your theory of how the problem occurs, and therefore, by extension, it suggests ways to improve the situation. Articulating this theory helps you to focus your question on the most important parts of the policy problem: *the mechanisms.* In the example, high CO_2 emissions trapped in the atmosphere are the essence of your theory. If animal methane only contributes a small amount to total CO_2 levels, focusing your solutions on reducing animal methane is not likely to do much to prevent sea level rise. Later in the Launch Process, when you fill out the Policy Solution Change Wheel, you will want to draw out your causal model or models for the interventions you will analyze. Causal models of policy problems serve another function as well: They quickly communicate to others your assumptions about the policy problem. This directs conversation to the core of the problem as you see it, allowing others to either embellish your model or argue with it, educating you further about the policy problem.

Why? The "Why?" question of the Wheel refers to why the policy problem needs to be improved—that is, it asks about the outcomes that will be achieved by a change in policy. Outcomes are usually described along a continuum, from more to less. The most obvious outcomes are those that specify a reduction in the policy problem: less homelessness, fewer workers without health care, or fewer illiterate children. However, outcomes can take other forms as well. Outcomes can refer to costs of current policies. For example, the question may focus on less expensive ways to shelter the homeless. Outcomes can concern equity issues such as reduced pay disparity for women. Finally, outcomes can point to freedoms or rights, such as safeguarding a community's right to be protected from environmental hazards.

As you continue your policy research, you should strive to be as specific as possible about how much improvement in outcomes you expect to achieve through policy change. For example, "How can we reduce the number of homeless people in our community by 10 percent" is better than simply asking for ways to reduce or eliminate homelessness. There are two reasons why specifics are better. First, specific outcome improvements provide criteria by which you can know whether the goals have been achieved. Second, a specific target can motivate decision makers. Eliminating homelessness may seem to decision makers an unrealistic goal that is not worthy of their attention. But an achievable 10 percent reduction may better capture their interest in your research.

Why Not? The "Why Not?" question of the Wheel is just as important as the "Why?" "Why Not?" refers to possible reasons for not trying to fix the policy problem. That is, "Why Not?" asks about the risks of negative consequences—side effects—from efforts to make things better. It asks about situations where the cure is worse than the disease. As you familiarize yourself with the policy problem, jot down these risks as you come across them. You may find reports of bad outcomes that occurred when people made well-intentioned policy changes to fix the policy problem. For example, increased police effort to arrest marijuana users may push marijuana users underground, exposing them to the hazards of black-market purchasing and more dangerous drugs. Or efforts to seed clouds to relieve drought may cause excessive flooding and erosion. Or capping CO_2 emissions may harm economic activity and increase unemployment. Documenting these risks will eventually help you design better interventions and implementation tactics.

In Table 2.1, we provide examples of Policy Problem Change Wheels for global warming and homelessness.

Now that you know the elements of the Policy Problem Change Wheel, it is time to begin gathering information to fill in the spokes of the Wheel. There are two stages in your information gathering. In this Launch Phase of the policy research effort, the focus is on getting an overview of what is known about the policy problem. In the next phase (Synthesize Existing Evidence, as covered in Chapter 3), you do a much more detailed analysis of the evidence.

The most useful sources for getting an overview of what is known about a policy problem are independent and impartial agencies that generate white papers on the policy problem. For policy problems of concern to private businesses, industry analysis firms (such as Forrester or Gartner) and general business magazines (see Table 2.2, Row A) often provide helpful descriptions of the business policy problem and interventions that have been tried and succeeded elsewhere. When the policy problem is one for which governmental and nongovernmental organizations are likely to take the lead, then different literature sources are useful (see Table 2.2, Row B). For example, for the topic of fostering economic development in Southeast Asia, you might review the following sources: The Association of Southeast Asian Nations (ASEAN) website, *The Economist,* the *Economic Outlook* from the Organization for Economic Co-operation and Development, and white papers generated by the United Nations Development Program (UNDP). This literature should be examined in a relatively cursory manner to get a feel for the types of evidence that are available about your policy problem and ways you might be able to refine and reframe your research question to make it more specific to focus on what is not yet known.

Reduce sources of global warming in the United States	What?	Reduce homelessness in developed countries
Reducing sources of global warming in countries other than the United States	What Not?	Reduce mental illness that may contribute to homelessness
United States	Who and Where?	Developed countries
Coal-burning power plants + gas-powered transport vehicles + animal methane emissions $\rightarrow CO_2$ emissions $\rightarrow$ warming	hoW?	Unemployment + mental illness $\rightarrow$ lack of financial, medical, and social support services $\rightarrow$ homelessness
Outcomes: economic costs of massive storms, economic cost of shoreline erosion	Why?	Outcomes: economic costs to local businesses, increased crime, human right to shelter
CO_2 auctions may encourage nonpolluters to pollute; efforts to cap emissions may harm the economy and employment opportunities	Why Not?	Some homeless people do not respond well to solutions that impose more structure on their lives

Table 2.1 Example Policy Problem Change Wheels

An important value of examining impartial literature sources is the identification of people sources who may be able to help you. If you find, for example, someone who authored reviews of the literature on the policy problem several years back, you may be able to contact the author to find out what has changed since then.

Therefore, for each source of information you surface, you are taking two actions. First, you are making notes using the Policy Problem Change Wheel about what is known and what is not as yet understood about the policy problem. Second, you are making notes about additional sources of information (people or documents) that may deepen your knowledge.

Activity 2.3 Familiarize Yourself With the STORM Context of the Policy Problem

A key spoke of the Policy Problem Change Wheel is the "Who and Where?" question, which we called the context of the policy problem. In this

Row	Audience	Sources for Finding Literature on Policy Problem
A	Business groups	*Information Week, Business Week, Financial Times, Management Information Systems Quarterly Executive, Academy of Management Perspectives, Sloan Management Review, Harvard Business Review, California Management Review*
B	Governmental and nongovernmental organizations	Magazines: *Foreign Affairs, Pacific Standard, Foreign Policy, The Atlantic, Harvard International Review, World Affairs, Harper's Magazine* Websites: The 4th Media, *Slate Magazine,* Council on Foreign Relations, Foreign Policy in Focus White Papers Developed By: General Accounting Office, National Academy of Sciences, National Research Council, Bureau of Labor Statistics, National Institutes of Health, Centers for Disease Control, World Bank, United Nations, European Union Commissions, The Association of Southeast Asian Nations (ASEAN), *The Economist,* Organization for Economic Co-operation and Development (OECD), and United Nations Development Program (UNDP)

Table 2.2   Examples of Literature Sources

activity, we describe context in more detail. By *context,* we mean the environment of conditions (including constraints and enablers), people (including implementers, decision makers, and affected people), organizations, and resources that affect a policy problem and will need to be considered if the policy problem is to be ameliorated. The context involves a number of different elements ranging from the social to the political and economic. It is important to become aware of all major elements in the context so that, later, you are not surprised by something you didn't consider. For example, if your policy problem concerns alcoholism on U.S. Indian reservations, and you ignored the economic context of the lack of jobs on reservations, you would fail the M2 test because your policy research study would not be comprehensive enough to be meaningful.

Because it is so important to comprehensively examine the various elements in the context, we use the mnemonic STORM for social conditions, technological conditions, organizational conditions, regulatory and legal conditions, and market conditions (Luo, Sun, & Wang, 2011). STORM is a vivid metaphor for the context of any policy problem, and we believe the acronym will help you remember to learn about these important elements of context when you familiarize yourself with a policy problem. We summarize the STORM context elements in Table 2.3.

STORM Context Elements	Definition	Example
Societal	Cultural, geographic, normative, community, or individual psychological or interpersonal issues	The psychological toll experienced by civil war refugees living in refugee camps
Technical	Any information or physical hardware, software, techniques, or work practices	The need for basic cell phone technology to be in place in order for mobile micro-banking to function properly
Organizational	Command and control structures, informal or formal influence mechanisms, task specializations, boundaries between subgroups, and how production happens within the formal and informal organizational structure of the corporations, communities, and families involved in the policy problem	The interorganizational memorandums of understanding between social service agencies may not be sufficient to prevent homeless people falling through service cracks
Regulatory	Clarity of distinctions between legal and illegal activities, strength of enforcement mechanisms, intentions underlying regulatory agency leadership and actions	The difficulty of distinguishing between legal and illegal copycat products contributes to counterfeiting in emerging economies
Market	Economic incentives that contribute to or reduce the policy problem; costs of doing nothing to ameliorate the policy problem	The lack of market competition among AIDS drug manufacturers influences the cost of AIDS drugs in developing countries

Table 2.3   Summary of STORM Context Elements

Filling out a version of Table 2.3 is helpful in keeping track of the elements of a policy problem's context. But simply knowing the contextual conditions is not enough. You have to identify whether the elements are aligned with each other. If all the STORM context conditions reinforce each other, whether they add to or subtract from the problem, we say they are aligned or operating in the same direction. For example, let's say your policy problem is the high rate of AIDS infections in a developing country. As you familiarize yourself with the STORM conditions, you become aware that, while technical, regulatory and market conditions are oriented in a direction that supports policy change, the social norms in the country discourage leaders from tackling the AIDS problem. This is a case of misalignment that may be a key barrier to successful policy change; this barrier may have to be addressed head-on. Other times, an element out of alignment may be the major ray of hope in a poor situation; to increase the chances of successful policy change, you may need to find ways to reinforce that element.

Activity 2.4 Conduct Policy Problem Stakeholder Analysis

Stakeholders are individuals, groups, and organizations that have a personal interest in the policy problem or its solution. Stakeholders can help or hinder your efforts to solve a policy problem, so at the very least, you'll need to understand their views. And if you can engage the views of key stakeholders in your policy research project, you can increase your chances of success. So you need to make sure that you have a comprehensive list of major stakeholder groups.

You probably identified the most important groups of stakeholders through your familiarization process. Make a list and jot down the roles they play in the policy problem. For example, actual or potential malaria victims may be the target of your proposed interventions, and nongovernmental organizations may be potential sources of funding for an intervention, such as bed nets.

To make sure you have a comprehensive list of stakeholder groups, you should ask yourself the following set of questions about the list:

- Does your stakeholder list include the focal unit of your analysis (recipient or target of policy change)? The *focal unit* is the individual, group, organization, and so on that is the primary focus of the policy research process. For example, for the problem of malaria in Zambia, you may decide that the focal stakeholder unit is the city with a high incidence of malaria because urban density contributes to the spread of infection and because city government is a good way to manage likely interventions (e.g., spraying mosquitos, eliminating stagnant water, distributing bed nets) that are likely to be made. City leaders or health care agencies may be the most appropriate organizations to represent this focal unit.

- Does your list include people who have authority or influence over the focal units? You can use the two-levels-up rule of thumb from systems theory to identify these stakeholder groups. For example, cities are included in regional councils or units of government, which in turn are influenced by national government. These higher levels of government are stakeholder groups that should be considered in your analysis.

- Does your list include important subgroups within the focal units? Here, you can use the two-levels-down rule of thumb. Within cities are neighborhoods with councils and clinics that may be able to help with the interventions. Within neighborhoods are families of individuals who are both the people at risk of contracting malaria and also people whose behavior will be key to the success of any intervention.

- Does your list include "customers," for instance, organizations and people who depend on the focal unit for goods or services? In the case of Zambia cities, one possibly important customer group might be the businesses that employ residents. These employers may have knowledge and resources that can help solve the problem. (Some customer groups could create barriers to change.)

- Does your list include "suppliers," who provide necessary goods and services to your focal unit? Important suppliers to malaria-infected cities are regional health workers and foreign drug companies.

- Does your list include "regulators," that is, groups other than those already considered that set rules or manage resources relevant to the policy problem? In the malaria case, regulators may include nongovernmental organizations, charities, and foundations of many sorts.

Once you've identified the stakeholder groups, you need to understand their stakes in, or views about, the problem. Sometimes, you will be able to do this just through your familiarization process; however, because you will want to engage them in your research, you will need to meet representatives of key groups and talk to them. You can't ask, "What is your causal model of the problem?" But you can find out what they think the problem is, what causes it, and what can be done about it. You may have some surprises! For example, you may learn that village heads do not see malaria as a problem—it's just part of the natural order of things.

You should expect to find differences of opinion across stakeholder groups. Part of your role as a policy researcher is to become aware of these differences, to pinpoint them in your causal model if they occur, and try to find common ground. If, for example, one view is that dams are the problem for creating stagnant water and another view focuses on lack of proper sanitation, you may find common ground by focusing on local water resources. Once you identify where interests intersect, you can reframe your policy research question on the areas of intersection.

Given the potentially large number of stakeholder groups, you may not be able to find an area of intersection for all. But you may be able to draw in a majority. It is now time to assess the extent of stakeholder agreement with your reframed policy research question. In this assessment, you should rate the stakeholder groups in terms of their support for the direction of your research and their ability to influence decisions and resources. Figure 2.3 shows an example of such an assessment. If, after completing this assessment, you conclude that there is little support for your policy research study, you may decide to reframe the policy question yet again. Or you may go ahead anyway because you believe that your research will give a voice to underrepresented groups. Perhaps, after you have collected more evidence, you will be able to engage additional stakeholders.

The hypothetical example in Figure 2.3 focuses on the policy problem of global warming. In this assessment, you have identified members of U.S. Congressional committees as the key decision makers concerning U.S. global warming. Six other stakeholder groups have positions about this policy problem, with varying degrees of influence over the decision makers. The influence or power of each group over the key decision makers is illustrated in the diagram by the relative distance between the decision maker and the stakeholders. The closer the stakeholder is to the decision maker in the diagram, the greater the stakeholder's power is. In the example, coal-burning facilities and auto manufacturers have more influence over the decision makers than environmental groups or alternative fuel suppliers. The pluses and minuses in the figure indicate the level of support for or opposition to the policy change. The stakeholders on the right side of the picture (auto manufacturers, coal-burning plants, and large cattle farmers) strongly oppose viewing global warming as a problem warranting policy change. In contrast, environmental groups, alternative fuel suppliers, and concerned scientists strongly advocate taking steps to reduce global warming and would be open to your research on alternative policy changes. Through an assessment like that in Figure 2.3, you can begin to learn whether there will be enough support for your policy recommendations and enough resources to implement them. In this hypothetical example, the prospects appear dim.

If your stakeholder analysis reaches a similar conclusion, you have a choice. You can continue to study the problem in the hopes your research will be so compelling as to remove opposition (the I'll-study-it-anyway approach). Or

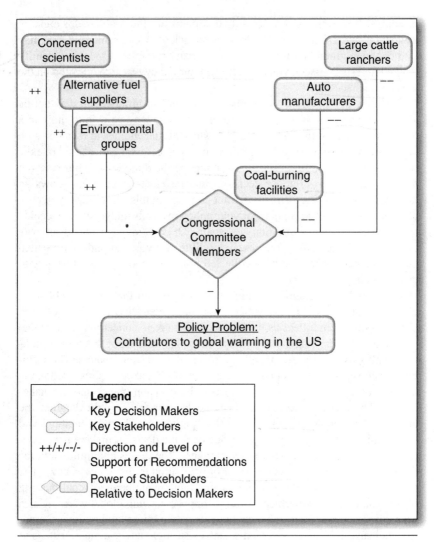

Figure 2.3 Policy Problem Stakeholder Analysis

you can reframe the policy research question in ways that may overcome stakeholder opposition (the let's-compromise approach). For policy problems like the one in Figure 2.3, compromise may not be achievable, but it often can be if you focus on common ground.

Activity 2.5 Identify and Engage Experts

To identify experts to speak with, look at the literature you've compiled for repeatedly mentioned organizations and frequently cited authors. For example, if you are interested in better agricultural practices in Southeast Asian countries, expert organizations include the United States Agency for International Development, the Peace Corps, and the World Bank, as each organization has published papers about these practices. Authors of an organization's papers on the topic are likely to be its experts.

Contact these experts, asking for short informational interviews. Test your understanding of what is already known about the problem and what is not known (in terms of the six spokes in the Policy Problem Change Wheel). Ask about the alternative interventions that have been considered and thrown away, surprises from past experiences dealing with the problem, negative side effects, what worked and where, and what didn't work and possible reasons. Ask them what they would focus on if they were to undertake a new policy research study on the problem. If the interview goes well, ask them if they would be interested in helping you in the future.

Remember that some of the people you are interviewing will have taken strong positions in favor of one solution over another. These positions don't mean you should not include them in your interviews. However, you should keep in mind the need to test their conclusions in light of your own research evidence.

Activity 2.6 Formulate Initial Policy Solution Options

Up to now, you have focused primarily on familiarizing yourself with the policy problem, including your Policy Problem Change Wheel, the STORM context of the policy problem, and stakeholders' causal models about the problem. It is now time to pull together this information more systematically to identify the set of solutions that you will need to evaluate. You should list possible solutions related to your causal model, either because they change the conditions that created or sustain the problem or because they change the mechanisms connecting initial conditions to outcomes. Possible solutions (also called *interventions*) you might consider for the malaria problem include removing dams on rivers, improving sanitation, spraying mosquito larvae, supplying mosquito nets, moving villages, offering alternative medical treatments, and so forth. The range of interventions you plan to evaluate should pass the M2 test by being manageable for you and meaningful for the policy makers. They should also be interventions that are relevant to the stakeholders you have engaged.

Next, you should organize what you know about the interventions using a Policy *Solution* Change Wheel. The Policy Solution Change Wheel is similar to the Policy Problem Change Wheel in Activity 2.2, except that you now take the interventions as your "What?" question instead of the general policy problem.

The Policy Solution Change Wheel asks you to answer a series of short questions about the intervention. Answering the "What?" question means describing the interventions themselves. The "What Not?" question identifies interventions that you are deliberately leaving out of further analysis. "Who and Where?" calls for you to describe the STORM context specifically for the interventions (e.g., geographic location, culture, timeframe) including the people who will be the direct focus of the interventions. "hoW?" describes the ways in which the interventions are believed to work; it provides the causal model or theory of the interventions. Note that different interventions may have different causal models. In addition, as discussed in Chapter 3, any intervention may have several competing theories. Try to keep track of these variations as you encounter them. "Why?" refers to the outcomes that the interventions are expected to achieve and therefore to the reasons the interventions should be implemented. Finally, "Why Not?" points to risks that must be minimized when implementing the interventions. These questions specific to a Policy Solution Change Wheel are shown in Figure 2.4.

As an example of the use of the Policy Solution Change Wheel, Bristol (2007) examined the rate of AIDS infections among women in sub-Saharan Africa, as Africa shoulders 24 percent of the worldwide AIDS-affected population yet carries only 3 percent of the global health work force ("Who and Where?"). New interventions were clearly needed based on the evidence that billions of dollars had been contributed to a system where only 28 percent of AIDS patients actually received the antiretroviral drugs needed to survive ("Why?") and that, to protect the progress that had been made in AIDS reductions, simply redirecting funding away from underdeveloped nations was not appropriate ("Why Not?"). Therefore, the focus of health care interventions for HIV/AIDS had to change from pumping money from foreign investors and donors into the existing system of aid ("What Not?") to focusing treatments on AIDS prevention. The intervention recommended behavioral changes and shifts in long-standing patterns of poverty and gender inequality ("What?"). The concept underlying the intervention was that, if local leadership was able to modify behaviors associated with gender inequality, fewer women would be exposed to AIDS-infected men ("hoW?").

An example of a Policy Solution Change Wheel for reducing tuberculosis in a rural region is shown in Figure 2.5.

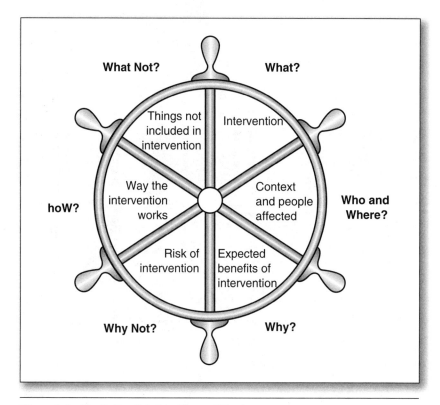

Figure 2.4   The Policy Solution Change Wheel

LAUNCH PHASE DELIVERABLES

Two deliverables are generated in the Launch Phase: your reframed policy research question and accompanying assessments (2.1) and a roster of advisers (2.2). In preparing these deliverables, remember the two tracking indicators. Both deliverables should meet the M2 test and engage stakeholders.

Deliverable 2.1 Reframed Policy Research Question

It is time to document what you've learned about the policy problem before you forget. We are not big believers in creating large reports that sit on shelves. But being effective in policy research involves a tremendous amount of communication—and much of that will be in concisely written memos and presentations using diagrams and visual aids as much as possible. Capturing

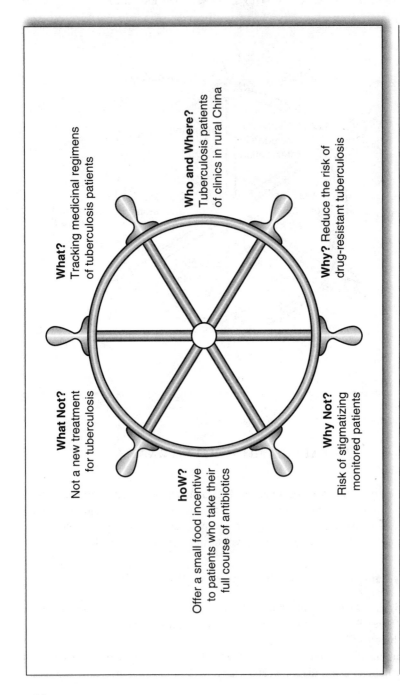

Figure 2.5 Policy Solution Change Wheel for Reducing Tuberculosis

your initial understanding of what is known about your selected policy problem in a short memo is very helpful to those you are working with, particularly when the memo is coupled with appendices containing the Policy Problem Change Wheel, Policy Problem STORM Conditions Table, Policy Problem Stakeholder Analysis, Policy Solution Change Wheel, and Policy Solution STORM Conditions Table. The outline for the memo can follow a general template, such as this:

1. Introduction:
   a. Initial research question (the one you started with at the beginning of the Launch Phase)
   b. Policy makers for whom the study is being done

2. Approach:
   a. Literature sources, stakeholders, and experts you consulted about the policy problem

3. Analysis:
   a. Policy Problem Change Wheel and causal model(s)
   b. STORM context alignment analysis
   c. Stakeholder analysis results about policy problem

4. Conclusions:
   a. Reframed research question focusing on topics not well understood
   b. Initial set of interventions (policy problem solutions) you will evaluate further (and ones you will not evaluate further)
   c. Policy Solution Change Wheel and causal model(s)

Deliverable 2.2 Roster of Advisers

A way to facilitate stakeholder engagement and consensus building among stakeholders is to involve them in your policy research process. Every policy research process should have a set of advisers. Advisers should be people who represent key stakeholder groups as well as experts. The size of the group doesn't matter. They don't have to meet altogether in person either. They don't even have to necessarily publicly announce their affiliation with you. If you are working for a nongovernmental organization or a senator, however, it may be politically useful to have a formally designated advisory board that actually meets as a body periodically because this can confer legitimacy on your policy research effort. In addition, if the composition of this board is bipartisan, it can help convince others that your policy research process is unbiased.

The primary responsibility of advisers is to talk with you informally throughout the policy research process and give you feedback as you generate plans, conclusions, and recommendations. The best advisers are knowledgeable and care about the policy problem and its potential solutions, are open-minded, and are willing to mentor you. Knowledgeable advisers are ones with prior policy research experience in the domain (for example, they may have written reviews or conducted research in the policy domain), ones with lived experience of the policy problem (such as a victim of spousal abuse for a study of domestic violence), and ones who can provide services or fund research or interventions. However, not all knowledgeable people are open-minded. Try to avoid selecting advisers who strongly advocate a single solution; instead, choose advisers who are genuinely interested in learning more about the problem.

The best advisers are busy people. What can you offer them in exchange for their advice and time? You can give the advisers credit for helping you and offer them the opportunity to jointly author the report if they are interested. You can discuss your conclusions with them before you share them with others. You can thank them for their help. Finally, you can offer them the opportunity to network with your other advisers. This can be especially valuable for advisers on business policy problems. Orchestrating occasions where people can share ideas—either through the telephone, via the Web, or in person—often provides a major motivation for advisers to participate.

The role of an advisory group is not simply to provide advice. Perhaps an even more important objective is to achieve what is called *buy-in*. When stakeholders buy in to your research, it is because they have had an opportunity to provide input and shape the direction of the research in ways that better address their concerns. Buy-in does not mean that participating stakeholders on an advisory board agree to anything you might propose. Rather, it means that they support the research because they have worked on it with you. In sum, having a roster of advisers can help by providing expert knowledge, access to other resources, and political support.

CONCLUSIONS

The initial policy research question will often be set for you by others. But you should not simply assume that this is best way to frame your research. The research question is vitally important because it focuses your attention and sets boundaries on what you consider. This chapter aimed to empower you to reframe the question that will guide the rest of your research journey. The Launch Phase is the time for you to learn enough about the policy problem to frame a good question. The Policy Problem Change Wheel and STORM content alignment analysis help you consider a full range of issues affecting your policy problem and its possible solutions. Stakeholder Analysis and Policy Solution Change Wheel analysis help you understand how various groups are likely to react to your eventual recommendations. Altogether, the steps of the Launch Phase help you frame a research question focused on what is not yet known, but needs to be known, to find a good solution to the policy problem. Engaging stakeholders is critical to this process.

You'll know you've done your best if you are able to start the next phase of the journey—Synthesize Existing Evidence—with a meaningful and manageable policy research question, with an understanding of the policy situation that is sensitive to alignment among the STORM context conditions, and with stakeholders who are engaged in subsequent phases of the policy research process.

EXERCISES

1. For a policy area of your interest (e.g., homelessness, water irrigation, global warming) identify at least five website that provide information that is likely to be helpful to you in familiarizing yourself with the problem. Do the organizations that host the sites have clear biases for (or against) a particular set of solutions? How can you tell? (What is your evidence for this conclusion?)

2. For a given policy problem, identify at least five key stakeholders and explain the nature of their stakes.

3. Identify at least five experts in the policy domain, describe the sources and nature of their expertise, and explain how you identified them.

4. For a given policy domain, generate at least five different policy research questions. How many Wheel spokes and STORM context elements are covered in each question? In the set of questions? Which of the questions do you think are better (more meaningful and manageable) than others, and why?

3

Synthesize Existing Evidence

SUMMARY

During the Launch Phase, you familiarized yourself with the policy problem and reframed the policy research question with the help of your advisers. Now, it's time to try to answer that question based on the best evidence you can find. In this phase, you assemble others' research on the policy question, summarize the findings, and synthesize them to come up with your best assessment of what is known about the answer. You also decide how confident you are in the answer and what important questions remain unanswered or uncertain. Synthesizing the existing evidence can be challenging but critical to the success of the entire policy research process because syntheses of evidence are often the basis on which policy recommendations are made and successfully justified. If, at the end of the Synthesize Existing Evidence Phase, you are highly confident in the conclusions you can draw, you may be able to proceed directly to the design of policy recommendations as discussed in Chapter 5. If, however, you do not have sufficient evidence or confidence in the evidence to support policy recommendations, your next step will be to obtain new evidence, as described in Chapter 4. The two activities and two deliverables of the Synthesize Existing Evidence Phase are shown in Figure 3.1. Next, we discuss the indicators you can use to track your progress in this phase.

INDICATORS TO TRACK YOUR COURSE

You can track your progress through the Synthesize Existing Evidence Phase by how well you know the existing evidence related to your reframed policy research question and by how well you can assess the strength of the existing evidence (because that tells you how confident you can be in the conclusions you draw from the existing evidence). These two indicators are discussed next.

Tracking Indicator 3.1 Knowledge of the Evidence

When you familiarized yourself with the policy area in the Launch Phase, you came across many different kinds of information, including opinions and theories for which no evidence was provided. Now, it's time to focus on the existing evidence, that is, relevant facts or data like actual events, people's self-reported experiences, and data produced by means of careful scientific observation. The collection of documents providing relevant data makes up the body of evidence for this phase of the policy research process. Not all documents providing evidence for your research will be equally relevant or equally high in quality. But you will need evidence, not just opinions and theories, to convince policy makers to accept your policy recommendations.

To develop your knowledge of the existing evidence, you will need skills in searching for documented evidence and in assessing the relevance and quality of the evidence. *Quality* here refers to a judgment (an opinion!) about the likelihood that the evidence reported in the document you review is unbiased, accurate, applicable, and verifiable. There are many indicators you can use to estimate the quality of evidence, such as its source (e.g., high-quality scientific journals versus general readership magazines), its author (independent versus sponsored by a party with vested interests), the procedures used to generate the evidence (e.g., controlled experiments versus unstructured observations or interviews), and thoroughness of documentation (e.g., detailed versus highly summarized reports with no details). For example, a report published in a

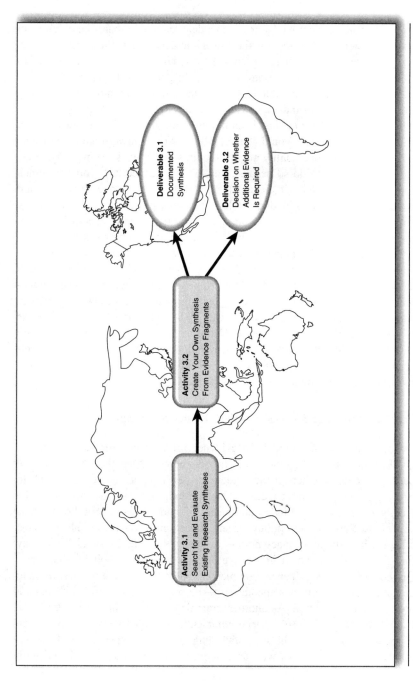

Figure 3.1 The Synthesize Phase Voyage Map

Activity 3.1
Search for and Evauate
Existing Research Syntheses

Activity 3.2
Create Your Own Synthesis
From Evidence Fragments

Deliverable 3.1
Documented
Synthesis

Deliverable 3.2
Decision on Whether
Additional Evidence
Is Required

reputable scientific journal by an independent, university-based research team that used facts and figures on the lower incidence of malaria infections in many African villages where insecticide-treated bed nets are used compared to those in which bed nets are not used would generally be viewed as high-quality evidence (Lengler, 2004). A magazine article written by someone who works for a chemical manufacturing company quoting a few people in one village who said that they had been bitten by mosquitoes less frequently as a result of using bed nets would generally be viewed as lower-quality evidence.

Assessing evidence quality always requires you to make some judgments, but it's important to do so because quality of evidence tells you how much confidence you can have in the conclusions you draw. However, it is important to understand that hard evidence relevant to your policy context may simply not exist. This does not mean you should not try to draw conclusions from fragmentary or lower-quality evidence. But you need to do so carefully.

The relevance of existing evidence is important because what counts as high-quality evidence will depend on the specifics of your policy research question. If your question is "Will treated bed nets help *prevent* malaria infections in the Amazon basin?" an article describing experiences with bed nets in one *African* village may be more relevant than a study about the effectiveness of various *treatments* for malaria infections throughout the Amazon basin. You may find yourself having to make many judgments about the quality and relevance of each piece of evidence you examine in the Synthesize Existing Evidence Phase of the policy research process.

Tracking Indicator 3.2 Assessment of Evidence Strength

Once you have assembled the evidence relevant to your policy research question (assessing the quality of each document along the way), you will need to decide whether all the evidence taken together is strong enough to support a policy recommendation. This is a judgment call, not just about the quality and relevance of individual pieces of evidence but about the evidence as a whole. Suppose your policy research question is "What would be the most effective information privacy policy for the state of Rhode Island?" You may find more evidence about ineffective policies than about policies that work. On the basis of this evidence, you may conclude that more evidence needs to be gathered—by you or someone else—before you can confidently make a policy recommendation. As another example, you may find strong evidence that telemedicine (the use of telecommunications technologies in the provision of medical services) enables accurate diagnoses in the specialties of dermatology and psychiatry as well as evidence that patients are satisfied with telemedicine, but you may still not be confident that telemedicine is cost-effective and comparable to face-to-face care for *orthopedic* care.

When you assess the strength of the body of evidence, you should take into account the quantity and consistency of evidence in addition to its quality and relevance. Do you have enough verification of the evidence to feel confident in the answer? Does all the evidence point in the same direction? Assessing the strength of the body of evidence is a bit like the decision of law enforcement personnel to prosecute a suspect for a crime. Detectives may be highly confident in their analysis of ballistics, fingerprints, and trace evidence, but attorneys may conclude the case as a whole is not strong enough to be prosecuted in court because the evidence does not implicate the suspect beyond a doubt.

In short, when you make policy recommendations, you want to be sure that you can support them with evidence. If the existing evidence is strong enough, you may feel confident to make recommendations straight away (Chapter 5). If not, you may want to recommend the collection of additional evidence on one or more very specific points (Chapter 4). Let's turn now to the activities that enable you to make judgments about the evidence.

SYNTHESIZE EXISTING EVIDENCE PHASE ACTIVITIES

The Synthesize Existing Evidence Phase has two activities:

Activity 3.1: Search for and Evaluate Existing Research Syntheses

Activity 3.2: Create Your Own Synthesis From Evidence Fragments

The starting point for the Synthesize Existing Evidence Phase is the deliverables you created during the Launch Phase. Without a carefully reframed policy research question, Problem and Solution Change Wheels (and theories or causal models of the problem and the interventions), and other tools like the STORM context conditions and Stakeholder Analysis, you will have great difficulty interpreting the evidence and assessing its quality, relevance, quantity, and consistency. For example, you may have found two high-quality studies that reach opposite conclusions about whether Head Start Programs help children later in life. Does this inconsistency mean the evidence as a whole is weak? Not necessarily—the two studies may have tested different theories or causal models of how the programs work. Depending on your theory, you may be justified in concluding that one of the studies is more relevant than the other. So it's important to do your homework in the Launch Phase so that you will be able to accomplish the goals of the Synthesize Existing Evidence Phase.

That said, the Synthesize Existing Evidence Phase is easiest when some-one else has already done much of the spadework for you. Therefore, your first order of business in this phase should be to locate and evaluate any published research syntheses on your policy question (Activity 3.1). You can think of a research synthesis as a study of published studies. As with primary research studies, research syntheses vary greatly in quality and relevance to your question. (And, if there are multiple syntheses, they may present different conclusions.)

If no published syntheses exist, it is probably because there is little evidence (few published studies) or because the evidence is primarily descriptive and qualitative; descriptive studies can be difficult to synthesize well. In that case, you will need to assemble and interpret whatever fragments of evidence do exist and determine whether you can use them to answer your research question (Activity 3.2).

Activity 3.1 Search for and Evaluate Existing Research Syntheses

Academic journals are good sources for papers reviewing existing evidence on various topics. However, the authors of review papers do not always have clear policy research questions to focus their conclusions, do not always use systematic or extensive procedures for selecting and evaluating evidence, and do not always report the procedures they used in conducting their reviews. On the assumption that more systematic procedures would increase the usefulness of and confidence in the results of research reviews for practical decision making, organizations such as the Cochrane Collaboration (in medicine) and the Campbell Collaboration (in education, criminal justice, and social welfare) were set up to coordinate and provide guidelines for how to do high-quality research syntheses, called *systematic reviews.*

The Cochrane Collaboration offers several specific recommendations for how to do systematic research reviews:

- Start with a clear and bounded policy question (usually about the effectiveness of a particular intervention).

- Search for relevant studies in many databases using a wide variety of search terms because researchers in different fields may have used different terms to describe the same thing.

- Look for unpublished studies as well as published ones because there may be biases against publishing studies that have negative findings (i.e., showing that an intervention had no effect) or studies that have the same findings as earlier studies (although these are important to practitioners because they may increase confidence that an intervention works).

- Evaluate individual studies carefully on the basis of the procedures used by the original researchers before deciding how much weight to put on the findings (e.g., studies with control groups and random assignment of subjects to treatments are often considered of higher quality than descriptive studies—although this is not always true, as we explain below).

These individual guidelines can be debated, but as a whole, you can use them to help you judge the quality of a systematic research synthesis. In addition, the guidelines will be very helpful if you have to do the synthesis entirely on your own.

Many policy fields, including business management, now provide support for the development and dissemination of systematic reviews in the belief that these reviews will help policy makers identify and implement evidence-based best practices (or at least better practices). Table 3.1 lists a few sources of systematic reviews.

As a result, you may find systematic research syntheses that can help you answer your policy research question. (Systematic reviews are usually published in academic journals, but the titles and abstracts of reviews can often be found on the websites of organizations like those listed in Table 3.1.) For example, in addition to many systematic reviews on medical treatments for malaria infections, there are also systematic reviews on nonmedical malaria prevention. As another example, you also can find several systematic reviews of the research on telemedicine. Table 3.2 provides brief summaries of four systematic reviews of research on telemedicine showing the policy question, how the authors sought and selected articles for detailed analysis, the number of articles analyzed relative to articles identified in the initial search, and conclusions drawn from the analysis (in addition to the possibility that there is a need for more research).

Published systematic reviews can be a starting point, but often they are not sufficient to support the kinds of policy recommendations that you will need to make. There are many reasons for this. The reviews may be out of date. Because of publication lags, a review published this year may not include research published in the last few years. In fields where the research activity is great, systematic reviews may need to be updated frequently to reflect the latest evidence. The reviews may also not address your specific policy question. For example, the reviews may cover effectiveness of an intervention for crime detection, when you are interested in the effectiveness of that intervention for crime prevention.

Source Title	Description
The Cochrane Collaboration in Healthcare (www.cochrane.org)	Assists patients, health-care providers, policy makers, and others in making well-informed decisions about heath care; composed of separate groups steered by one head group democratically elected and registered as a charity in the United Kingdom
The Campbell Collaboration (C2; www.campbellcollaboration.org)	Prepares, maintains, and synthesizes educational, criminal, judicial, and social welfare reviews; produces reviews of the effects of social intervention based on voluntary participation of researchers from various backgrounds
EPPI Centre: Evidence for Policy and Practice Information (eppi.ioe.ac.uk/)	Works to produce reviews dealing with education, health promotion, employment, social care, and crime and justice using collaborative partnerships; conducts training and workshops on systematic research synthesis
Center for Evidence-Based Crime Policy (CEBC) at George Mason University (gemini.gmu.edu/cebcp/)	Aims to make research a key aspect of decisions about crime and justice policies; develops translation tools in order to better communicate between research and practice
Jeffrey Pfeffer and Bob Sutton's Evidence-Based Management website (www.evidence-basedmanagement.com/)	Encourages experimentation and evolving by doing, and searching for the risks and drawbacks in what is recommended
Resources for Journalists at Harvard's Kennedy School (www.hks.harvard.edu/gateway/media)	Supplies high-quality and timely policy-oriented primary research by academic researchers on topics such as climate change, criminal justice, labor issues, corporations, and so on

Table 3.1   Example Sources of Evidence-Based Research

Another reason that an existing review may not be sufficient is that it may not address your context ("Who and Where?"). For example, the review may cover studies done in Africa, when your interest is the Amazon. In some cases,

Review	Mair and Whitten (2000)	Roine, Ohinmaa, and Hailey (2001)	Whitten et al. (2002)	Hersh et al. (2002)
Focus	Patient satisfaction	Patient outcomes, administrative changes, and economic assessments	Cost-effectiveness	Efficacy for making diagnostic and care management decisions
Study Search Strategy	Searches with 4 key words of 6 databases, with additional hand searches	13 different searches of databases, plus single searches of 6 other databases, plus consultations with experts and hand searches of reference lists	Multiple key-word searches of 6 databases	36 searches of 4 databases plus 10 supplementary searches
Study Selection Criteria (Included)	Clinical trials that examine patient satisfaction with teleconsultation	Scientific studies reporting outcomes and a comparison between a telemedicine alternative and a nontelemedicine alternative	Original research on telemedicine including cost-effectiveness data	Studies on 3 types of telemedicine situations (e.g., home based versus hospital based); studies that compare diagnostic or care management performance data in telemedicine situations with those of a control situation

(Continued)

Study Selection Criteria (Excluded)	Review or discussion papers, educational studies not linked to patient care, studies where patients were not present at either point of care	Noncontrolled and descriptive studies	Cost-benefit studies for education, hypothetical cost analyses or modeling with no clinical linkage, economic analysis with no substantiation for claimed resource use	Telemedicine situations that do not normally involve face-to-face care; low-tech (e.g., telephone-based) telemedicine; medical advice websites for the public
Number of Studies Analyzed	32 studies met selection criteria; only 7 studies reported covering more than 100 patients	1,124 studies dealing with telemedicine found; 133 articles obtained for closer inspection; 50 articles found to meet inclusion criteria; 34 articles assessed some clinical outcomes	612 articles, 557 without cost data, leaving 55 studies for analysis	4,367 possibly relevant articles; 59 studies fit the inclusion criteria
Conclusions	"Methodological deficiencies (low sample sizes, context, and study designs) of the published research limit the generalizability of the findings. The	"Evidence regarding the effectiveness or cost-effectiveness of telemedicine is still limited. Based on current scientific evidence, only a few telemedicine applications can be recommended for broader use." (p. 765)	"There is no good evidence that telemedicine is a cost-effective means of delivering health care." (p. 1434) "In large part, comparative cost-effectiveness of	"The strongest evidence for the efficacy of telemedicine . . . came from the specialties of psychiatry and dermatology. . . . Despite the widespread use of telemedicine in most major specialties, there is strong evidence in only a few of

studies suggest that teleconsultation is acceptable to patients in a variety of circumstances, but issues related to patient satisfaction require further exploration." (p. 1517) "Most studies have produced more questions than answers. Thus far, most telemedicine research has had a technological focus." (p. 1519)	"Decision makers who are under public and commercial pressure to start new telemedicine services should link the implementation of new, and in many cases costly, technology to realistic development of a business case and subsequent data collection and analysis." (p. 770)	telemedicine systems depends on the unique local aspects of the individual service being evaluated. A telemedicine service that is cost-effective in the remote highlands of Scotland is unlikely to generate the same cost-effectiveness in the middle of Manchester. . . . It is important to recognize that a service may be highly clinically and cost-effective in one context but highly ineffective when transferred to another context in which accessibility and quality of local services are far higher." (p. 1436)
		them that the diagnostic and management decisions provided by telemedicine are comparable to face-to-face care." (p. 197) "One anomalous finding was that store-and-forward teledermatology appears to have better diagnostic capability than interactive teledermatology. The most likely explanation is that the store-and-forward study used good-quality static images, whereas the best interactive study used video images of lower spatial resolution." (p. 206)

Table 3.2 Summaries of Four Systematic Reviews in the Area of Telemedicine

even the "When?" of the studies covered in a review may be seen as problematic support for current policy recommendations, perhaps because the studies involve older technologies. For example, a systematic review of research on environmental management (e.g., swamp drainage) for malaria prevention found that most studies had been conducted prior to the Global Malaria Eradication Campaign of 1955 to 1969 and therefore relied heavily on studies conducted in the first quarter of the 20th century (Keiser, Singer, & Utzinger, 2005). Even if you are willing to accept the validity of evidence that old, appropriateness of context is also crucial! For example, the African Medical Research Foundation generally does not support environmental management for reducing malaria infections because the mosquito most responsible for malaria infections in equatorial Africa breeds easily in pools of rainwater that are not effectively prevented by drainage projects (African Medical and Research Foundation, 2006).

Reviews may also not address specific issues that you need to understand to make convincing recommendations, such as why an intervention works, its potential negative side effects, and necessary implementation factors (e.g., funding, organizational support, training). You often need this information to win over policy makers to support your proposals.

Finally, the reviews may reveal just how little good evidence exists to support a convincing policy recommendation. A look at Table 3.2 shows how few studies may provide relevant information and how inconclusive the body of studies can be, even when there are very many studies in a policy domain. (What recommendations would you make based on the conclusions presented in Table 3.2?)

So what do you do if there are no systematic reviews on your policy question, or if you don't believe the existing reviews are adequate to support the kind of policy recommendations you need to make? If no systematic reviews are available on your topic, it could be a sign that there are very few primary research studies on your policy question. For example, there may be only a handful of published studies on the effectiveness of information *privacy* policies. In a case like this, you don't have to give up: You may be able to draw useful conclusions from closely related research, such as research on the effectiveness of information *security* policies.

Alternatively, there may be no studies of the sort that are easily synthesized using the guidelines commonly given for systematic reviews (e.g., studies with quantitative measurements of outcomes in comparison with control groups), but there may be any number of detailed observational studies (e.g., case studies, interview studies) describing individual situations in which an intervention was implemented. Observational studies are common in many areas of social policy research because the interventions are typically complex and highly tailored to the local context. Such studies are more difficult to synthesize than comparative studies, but doing so may actually tell you more about what you need to know to design recommendations that are appropriate for your context. This is where Activity 3.2 comes in. Activity 3.2 involves crafting your own research synthesis from existing fragments of evidence.

Activity 3.2 Create Your Own Synthesis From Evidence Fragments

To make use of fragmentary and possibly lower-quality evidence, it is particularly useful to start with your theory or causal model of the intervention (see Chapter 2), that is, a model of how and why the intervention is believed to work (bring about the desired outcomes). For instance, there are at least four different theories that explain why early childhood development programs, such as Head Start, help children do better in school over the long term with fewer social and health problems (e.g., drug dependency). The programs are said to succeed because they (1) improve children's cognitive and intellectual performance; or (2) improve children's social competence and social interaction skills; or (3) increase children's use of preventive health screenings and medical care, which can lead to early detection and correction of problems that would hinder learning; or (4) provide a supportive home environment with parental participation in children's learning, which helps with cognitive performance, social skills, and health (Anderson et al., 2003). Different theories like these are important for a number of reasons. For one, they may explain inconsistent findings across studies—and knowing that may give you greater confidence in your conclusions. In addition, they may suggest different interventions or variations on an intervention that will help it work better in your context. Finally, they can force you to reconsider your own theories—after all, your recommendations will only be as good as the theories they are based on, so take advantage of the opportunity to consider alternatives! Part of your work as a policy researcher is to use the existing evidence to sort out which theory provides the best explanation of the problem or why an intervention works so that your policy recommendations will be sound.

Sometimes, the only evidence you can find on a topic is a few case studies. Case studies often make up in their rich detail for the fact that they only examine one or a few individual cases. If you find yourself in that situation, read each case study carefully and assess whether the study provides evidence related to elements of your Policy Solution Change Wheel, including alternate theories of the intervention, if they exist. To do this systematically, you'd probably want to create a template like the one in Table 3.3 for making notes about each case study you read. In this hypothetical example, the notes deal with (1) the "Who and Where?" of the case because that helps you assess relevance, (2) any outcomes reported ("Why?") that relate to the four alternative theories ("hoW?") you are investigating, (3) comments about actions taken when implementing the intervention ("What?") that might be good things to add to your recommendations, and (4) your assessment of study quality. You don't want to write just *yes* or *no* in the columns. You should actually summarize information in the study that led you to conclude that a pathway was (or was not) important or that there was no evidence one way or the other.

Category of Information Sought From Each Case Study	Example Case Study, Date
Context ("Who and Where?")	Saint Louis, MO, 90 children, mainly Latino
Outcomes reported (positive and negative), e.g., higher graduation rates, dropping out of the program	12 years after the program, all but 5 of the students were still in school and not on academic probation
Any evidence that children in the program had better cognitive performance?	No evidence
Any evidence that children in the program had better social skills?	Students were observed before and after the program and found to interact better in ways that did not seem only due to age
Any evidence that children in the program took advantage of health screenings?	No evidence
Any evidence that parents of the children in the program were more involved in their education?	Parents visited the classroom frequently and were reported to have read to their children weekly
Implementation issues	A weekly support group was held for parents
Assessment of study quality	High

Table 3.3   Sample Template for Synthesizing Case Studies on Early Childhood Development Programs

There are a few things to keep in mind when creating and filling out templates like the one in Table 3.3. First, you should tailor the template to your research question and your Policy Solution Change Wheel, including alternative theories of the intervention, if present. No standard template will work for all policy research. Second, when you summarize the outcomes, you should avoid noting only things that went well. You should also note things that did not change, even though they were expected to, and you should pay particular attention to unintended effects, especially negative ones, because they may indicate why you should not do the intervention ("Why Not?"). But happy surprises are worth noting, too, because they may suggest additional reasons for adopting your recommendations! Third, you may also want to make notes about anything unique about the intervention or the way that it was implemented that might have affected the outcome. Examples of possibly important implementation factors include the nature and quality of the physical setting (e.g., cheerful, dilapidated), the kind of technology used, if any (e.g., computers, special games), additional training and support, rewards for good performance, and so on. This type of information can give you powerful clues about why an intervention may work in some settings but not in others and about whether the intervention can be successfully adapted to work in your context. Lastly, as discussed more below, you probably want to include an estimate of the quality of each study to make sure that you give it as much weight as it is due (but not more).

The fragments-of-evidence approach was used to assess the effectiveness of Megan's Law, which established a registry of convicted sex offenders and notified the community of the presence of such offenders in an effort to help to prevent re-offense (Pawson, 2006). The policy researcher who conducted a research synthesis on Megan's Law did not find enough studies of the sort that would lend themselves to a conventional systematic review; for instance, there were few studies that compared the re-offense rate of registered offenders with that of a control group. (One study found no significant difference in re-offense rate but did find that repeat offenders were arrested more quickly for new sex offenses.) However, the policy researcher found a large number of studies focusing on different aspects of this policy domain.

Despite the lack of any coherent body of evidence, the policy researcher was able to piece together fragments gleaned from many studies of varying quality, focused on different aspects of the problem, using different methodologies (Pawson, 2006). This piecing together of evidence fragments led the researcher to conclude that the results of implementing Megan's Law were not entirely as intended. Members of the public, law enforcement personnel, and repeat offenders do not always behave as expected by the theory of the intervention. Great differences exist across states in the implementation of each step of the process (registration, notification, community response, offender response), and details of the implementation of each step have important consequences all the way through the process. Table 3.4 shows the differences discovered between the theory of the implementation as expected in Megan's Law and the theory of implementation as actually practiced.

The fragments-of-evidence approach can also be applied when research about interventions that succeed in solving a problem is almost completely absent. For instance, one policy researcher noted that current models of

How the Law Should Work	How the Law Actually Worked
Registry: Upon release from jail, all sex offenders should be registered in a database	Record keeping in offender registries varies greatly; law enforcement personnel have difficulty keeping registries up to date (particularly the offenders' addresses, which is critical information for timely community notification); identifying high-risk repeat offenders is hard to do well
Notification: When the offenders move into a community, law enforcement personnel should notify citizens about the released offenders living in their communities	Community notification approaches vary greatly (different media; some approaches active, some approaches passive); there appear to be tradeoffs between providing adequate information to vulnerable people and the risk of harassment of released offenders
Surveillance: Community members should help law enforcement personnel monitor suspicious behavior by registered offenders	Law enforcement personnel spend enormous amounts of time and effort monitoring released offenders; harassment of offenders occurs frequently, although estimates of its severity vary
Offender Compliance: Community surveillance should "shame" potential repeat offenders, decreasing the likelihood that they will re-offend	Offender compliance with registration is far from perfect; public surveillance may hinder treatment; the effect of shaming on repeat offenses is still unknown

Table 3.4   Megan's Law—How the Law Should Work Versus Actually Worked

(Adapted from Pawson, 2006)

consumer information privacy protection do not work and need to be replaced (Culnan, 2011). Unfortunately, this conclusion by itself does not offer policy makers positive guidance on what to do. In this case, the policy researcher looked to security legislation and found that it offered a model (a theory of the intervention) that could be applied to information privacy protection. The theory of the intervention in this case was a six-step model of accountability and governance: (1) Write a formal policy about how the corporation will protect consumer privacy; (2) ensure executive oversight of compliance with the policy; (3) set up ongoing processes for risk assessment and mitigation; (4) conduct formal education and create awareness; (5) enforce the policy; and (6) ensure transparency and redress. Note that a theory of the intervention can be used both to craft new policy recommendations and to evaluate the effectiveness of the interventions after implementation.

When you use the fragments-of-evidence approach to synthesize evidence related to your policy question, keep two points in mind. First, if you use observational studies (e.g., case studies) as part of your evidence, be aware that the measurements of outcomes are qualitative rather than quantitative, and there are no control groups (groups that do not receive the intervention) against which the findings can be compared. Therefore, you should go out of your way to examine additional studies for corroboration or contradictions. Use the findings of one study to help you make sense of the findings of another. On the other hand, know that observational studies are generally much more valuable than experimental and quantitative research for providing information about context and implementation details.

A second point to keep in mind as you synthesize fragments of evidence is that the studies you assemble in your synthesis will not be uniform in quality, even if they use the same general research approach. For example, some case studies (1) may be published in the highest-quality peer-reviewed academic journals by independent researchers; (2) provide a wealth of detail about how concepts were operationalized and how the data were collected and analyzed; and (3) richly describe how the intervention was designed, implemented, and resulted in its outcomes. Other studies, while still offering some useful information, (1) may have been written by people who designed and implemented the implementation and therefore, possibly, may be biased in reporting its outcomes; (2) may have been published in magazines where articles are not subjected to careful critiques and requests for improvement; and (3) may be quite sketchy in providing important details. There is no reason to exclude lower-quality studies completely from your synthesis, especially if they happen to provide pieces of the mosaic that you cannot fill in from other sources. But you should not have as much confidence in the conclusions you draw from lower-quality studies as you do from those of higher quality.

The bottom line is that, when you decide a piece of lower-quality evidence is important for your synthesis, you should be much more cautious in how much weight you give it. If your policy recommendation is going to cost zillions of dollars and have a nontrivial risk of doing significant harm, you cannot rely on a single article that breezily describes how XYZ organization succeeded by doing something similar. This principle means that, when you summarize research in a template like Table 3.3, you should estimate the quality of each study (high, medium, or low) in terms of how verifiable the evidence is and how likely it is to apply in other contexts. And, in addition to estimating the quality of each piece of evidence in your synthesis, you should try to estimate the strength of the conclusions you draw from the entire body of evidence. Returning to the criteria mentioned earlier, the strength of your confidence in conclusions drawn from the entire body of evidence should depend not only on the average quality of the evidence but also on its quantity and consistency. If you have a vast quantity of medium-quality evidence that all points in the same direction, you may be willing to have greater confidence in your conclusions than if you have only one high-quality study or if you have six high-quality studies, three of which show good outcomes from an intervention, two of which show no change, and one of which shows adverse outcomes. It's a good idea to be explicit—at least to yourself—in how much confidence you are willing to place in the body of evidence supporting your policy recommendations. Table 3.5 suggests one set of criteria you can use for arriving at this judgment.

Strength of the Body of Evidence	Criteria
High	Many medium- to good-quality studies consistently suggest the same conclusion about some aspect of the policy problem or solution
Medium	The preponderance of evidence suggests a particular conclusion, but the evidence is sparse, of medium to low quality, or contains significant inconsistencies (i.e., a few studies strongly contradict the general consensus)
Low	There are few relevant studies, the evidence is generally of poor quality, or the findings are highly inconsistent

Table 3.5   Criteria for Evaluating Strength of the Body of Evidence About Your Policy Question

SYNTHESIZE PHASE DELIVERABLES

The deliverables of the Synthesize Existing Evidence Phase include documentation of what you have learned from the body of evidence (Deliverable 3.1) and a decision (Deliverable 3.2) either to obtain new evidence on particular points (discussed in Chapter 4) or to proceed directly to the design of policy recommendations (discussed in Chapter 5).

Deliverable 3.1 Documented Synthesis

As we explained in Chapter 2, we are not fond of documentation for its own sake. But there are several reasons that you should take the time to document both the process and the results of your research synthesis. First, quite practically, you don't want to forget them. You have done a lot of work to get to this point, and it is very easy to forget important details. If questions come up later, you will want to be able to answer them without reconstructing your work. Don't just shove all the papers you read into a drawer (or onto a flash drive); take the time now to pull all the information together into one document that you can consult later.

Second, your synthesis of the evidence may be very important later when you try to convince others that your proposed policy change is both doable and worth doing. Being able to point to other places where the intervention has been successfully tried is good. But showing how carefully you combed through the evidence and considered all the details is priceless when it comes to people who have grave concerns about the costs, benefits, and risks of your proposed policy change.

Third, suppose you design a policy change and then find (life happens!) that the economy turned sour, there's a change in administration, or your policy makers have another urgent priority. Now may not be the right time for the change you wish to see happen. But the time may come again when your policy change is possible. How much easier it will be for you to *update* your synthesis of the evidence than to *redo* it all from scratch!

Finally, suppose you implement your policy change, and it is successful. Others will come to you looking to learn what you did, why you did it, and whether it will work for them. Your synthesis of the evidence is one thing you can offer to help with their policy research process.

Deliverable 3.2 Decision on Whether Additional Evidence Is Required

The other output of the Synthesize Existing Evidence Phase is a decision about whether you know enough to develop policy recommendations (discussed in Chapter 5). This is the time to ask about gaps in your evidence-based knowledge about the effectiveness of various interventions for your policy problem and about the issues involved in implementing those interventions.

Consider the confidence you have in the body of evidence on your policy question. If you are not confident in your knowledge, you have three basic choices. First, you can go ahead anyway and hope for the best. We do not recommend this, but if the risks are low and the intervention is easily reversible, then you may want to go ahead. Second, you can abandon your project. Third, you can conduct (or commission someone else to conduct) a targeted primary research study to answer one or more specific questions to fill important gaps in your knowledge. The third choice is the topic of Chapter 4.

You do not have to, and probably should not try to, make this decision alone. This is a good opportunity to engage your advisers. Describe the process you went through to review the existing evidence systematically and what you learned from doing so. (You may even want to give your advisers a copy of your documented synthesis.) Ask for their input. Make the decision together about whether to proceed with a policy recommendation or additional research.

CONCLUSIONS

The Synthesize Existing Evidence Phase can be time-consuming and challenging, but it is critical to the success of your entire policy research project. It will help you design a successful policy change, and it will help you convince others that the policy change you recommend is both doable and worth doing.

EXERCISES

1. Look for a source of systematic reviews relevant to your policy interests. (See Table 3.1 for some sources and links to more sources.) Find a systematic review of interest to you. How was the review prepared? What conclusions were drawn? How confident are you in the conclusions drawn?

2. Is this systematic review up to date? Search for a recent primary study of the sort that would be included in an update of the systematic review.

Evaluate this new study from the perspective of the systematic review. Would it be included or excluded? If included, how do the findings square with the conclusions of the systematic review?

3. Select a research report from a think tank that does research relevant to your policy interests. (The report should provide evidence relating to the pros and cons of some intervention.) What are the potential sources of bias in this research? What procedures were followed in conducting the research? Are these procedures likely to have produced high-quality evidence? Read the report looking for evidence that the report exhibits political bias. (Hint: Did the report fairly consider both the pros and the cons of the intervention?) How much weight should you put on the report's conclusions?

4. Construct a Policy Solution Change Wheel for the intervention (or one of the interventions, if more than one) examined in the think tank report.

4

Obtain New Evidence

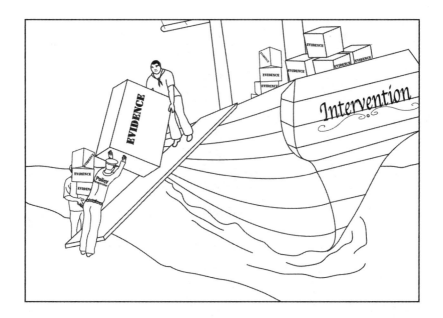

SUMMARY

This chapter describes how you can obtain new evidence if your systematic review (discussed in Chapter 3) leaves you with unanswered questions about either the problem or its effective solutions. In the Obtain New Evidence Phase, you design a plan for collecting and analyzing data to fill in missing pieces of your knowledge. You then manage data collection, whether or not you actually collect the data yourself. You start this phase with a research question that is typically much narrower and more targeted than the one you began with in the Launch Phase. After you define the key concepts in the question, you have a major choice to make: What kind of data will you use to answer the question? Although many policy researchers believe that using secondary data archives

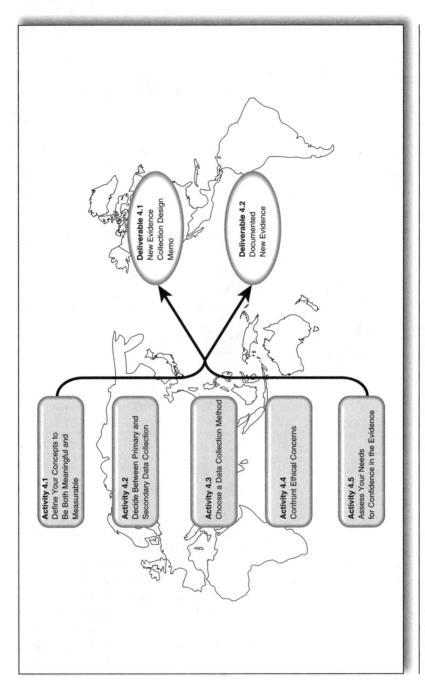

Figure 4.1 The Obtain New Evidence Phase Voyage Map

(databases assembled by others for purposes other than yours), such as U.S. Census Bureau data, our goal in this chapter is to encourage you to collect new primary evidence (or work with someone who will do it for you). The reason is that primary evidence often will give you greater confidence in your policy recommendations. High-quality, new primary evidence can be collected in various ways, including interviews, case studies, and field experiments.

We also discuss the ethical issues involved in obtaining new evidence. The five activities and two deliverables of the Obtain New Evidence Phase are shown in Figure 4.1.

Entire books have been written about each of these approaches, so we can give you only a basic overview here. Table 4.1 includes some of our favorite books on these topics. We encourage you create a library of reference works to support your policy research journey.

As usual, we start this chapter with indicators you can use to track your course through this phase.

- *Survey Research Design:* E. R. Babbie, Wadsworth, 1990

- *The International Handbook of Social Impact Assessment: Conceptual and Methodological Advances:* H. Becker & F. Vanclay, Edward Elgar, 2006

- *Learning More From Social Experiments: Evolving Analytic Approaches:* H. S. Bloom, Russell Sage Foundation, 2005

- *Applied Cost-Benefit Analysis:* R. J. Brent, Edward Elgar, 2008

- *Statistics in the Social Sciences: Current Methodological Development:* S. Kolenikov, D. Steinley, & L. A. Thombs, Wiley, 2010

- *Analyzing Policy: Choices, Conflicts and Practices:* M. C. Munger, W. W. Norton, 2000

- *Qualitative Research in Business and Management* (2nd edition), M. Myers, Sage, 2013

- *Experimental and Quasi-Experimental Design:* W. R. Shadish, T. D. Cook, & D. T. Campbell, Wadsworth, 2002

- *Secondary Data Analysis:* T. P. Vartanian, Oxford University Press, 2010

- *Statistical Analysis of Cost-Effectiveness Data:* A. R. Willan & A. H. Briggs, Wiley, 2006

- *Case Study Research: Theory, Methods, Practice:* A. G. Woodside, Emerald Group, 2010

- *Case Study Research: Design and Methods:* R. K. Yin, Sage, 2008

Table 4.1   Selected References on Policy Research Design

TRACKING INDICATORS FOR THE
OBTAIN NEW EVIDENCE PHASE

Obtaining new evidence requires you to design a data collection effort that will yield the evidence you need and then to manage data collection (whether you do it yourself or not) in a way that ensures your design is properly carried out. You can stay on track in this phase by following the guidance of your Policy Change Wheels and by staying flexibly focused on your targeted research question. Monitoring these indicators and making appropriate adjustments as necessary will help you obtain the new evidence that informs policy makers and motivates them to act.

Tracking Indicator 4.1 Adherence to the Policy Change Wheels

Designing a data collection effort involves decisions about data sources, what data to collect, how to ensure the validity and reliability of the data you collect and the conclusions you draw, and how to protect the people who provide data. Keeping the Policy Change Wheels in mind helps you make these decisions well. If you need to obtain new evidence about the policy problem, keep the Policy Problem Change Wheel in mind. If you need to obtain new evidence about one or more possible interventions, keep the Policy Solution Change Wheel in mind.

Keeping the Wheels in mind means that you should use the information you acquired when completing the Wheel in the first place. For example, if your Wheel indicates that the STORM context ("Who and Where?") element of geographic setting (urban ghettos vs. poor, rural districts) may make a difference in whether an intervention works, you will surely want to collect new evidence in the setting most relevant to you. If your Wheel indicates that ground water pollution is a possible "Why Not?" (unintended negative consequence) of your preferred intervention, you will definitely want to go out of your way to gather new evidence about this harmful outcome so that you do not make an irresponsible policy recommendation. Use the Policy Change Wheels as your constant guide for designing and managing new evidence collection.

Tracking Indicator 4.2 Flexible Focus on the Targeted Question

Change happens! It happens in life and it happens during policy research. Among the many changes that can affect your ability to carry out a new evidence collection effort and how you interpret its findings are changes in the people who make policy, breakthroughs in technology, new societal dynamics (new conflicts or wars), changes in legislation, and alterations in economic conditions, among others.

In policy research, you need to be much more adaptable to these changes than is typical in academic research. For example, a deteriorating economy may mean that you can no longer count on the support of a key stakeholder. You would obviously have to change your research plans. Or a newly elected policy maker may have different priorities than the former incumbent. You would obviously want to try to address the policy makers' needs. But you also need to avoid losing focus on your own objectives. Returning again and again to the targeted research question can prevent you from drifting while you make the inevitable adjustments in your plans. Remember that your advisers can be a great help to you in staying attuned to changing conditions and balancing the need for adjustments with your need to stay the course.

OBTAIN NEW EVIDENCE PHASE ACTIVITIES

The literature on principles of rigorous research design fills entire libraries. In this chapter, we focus on the design activities unique to policy research. The five activities in the Obtain New Evidence Phase of policy research are the following:

Activity 4.1: Define Your Concepts to Be Both Meaningful and Measurable

Activity 4.2: Decide Between Primary and Secondary Data Collection

Activity 4.3: Choose a Data Collection Method

Activity 4.4: Confront Ethical Concerns

Activity 4.5: Assess Your Needs for Confidence in the Evidence

Activity 4.1 Define Your Concepts to Be Both Meaningful and Measurable

At the end of the Synthesize Existing Evidence Phase, you may have found yourself missing important evidence about the policy problem, such as how frequently it occurs, the outcomes experienced by certain vulnerable groups, or "hoW?" it happens. Alternatively, you may have found yourself missing important evidence about possible solutions to the problem, such as whether a particular intervention has negative side effects or what additional steps must be taken to make the intervention work in your context. Either way, you should formulate a targeted research question to guide the Obtain New Evidence Phase. Then, you need to step back and think hard about the meaning of each noun and verb in your targeted research question.

Words like *poverty, crime,* and *health* or *improve, solve,* and *cure* can have many different meanings. If you use these words to mean one thing, and others interpret them differently, you will experience grave problems in your policy research career. Research associates will not collect the evidence you need, policy makers will misunderstand your recommendations, and you will talk at cross-purposes with your most important stakeholders. Consider a policy change to provide more funding for cancer research, and suppose the goal is presented in terms of finding a cure. Does cure mean treatment that drives cancer into remission? Does cure mean preventing cancer from occurring in the first place? Does it mean better quality of life for patients after surgery? To get your new evidence gathering off to a good start and keep it there, the first question you should answer is this: What exactly do you mean by your key concepts?

The more precisely you define the key concepts in your targeted question, the better you will be able to avoid misinterpretation. Let's say that your policy research question includes school performance. If you don't define that term, others may think you mean literacy rates in the community, dropout rates, or teacher qualifications, when you were actually thinking in terms of annual standardized test scores. If you define school performance as school children's scores on annual standardized tests, phrasing your targeted question in terms of annual standardized test scores will avoid miscommunication. If your definition of school performance is broader than standardized test scores, then you will need to state explicitly how you combine different metrics (scores and literacy rates and dropout rates) into your assessment of school performance. Failing to be explicit will confuse everyone and may even discredit you as a policy researcher.

Being specific and explicit does not mean oversimplification. Multiple indicators and a formula to combine them are often needed to measure complex concepts like school performance well. Check the existing literature on your policy area, and consult your advisers for suggestions for how to measure important concepts.

Operationalizing Key Concepts

The process of precisely defining and selecting measures for concepts is referred to as *operationalizing* the concept. For the policy research question "Do electronic medical records reduce private physicians' medical costs without harming quality of care?" four concepts need operationalization: *electronic medical records, private physicians, medical costs,* and *quality of care.* For example, you may define electronic medical records as the purchase and implementation of software developed to meet the guidelines of the U.S. government's health care reform bill. You might then measure use of electronic medical records in health care settings as the percentage of the doctors' work time spent using the software. Operational definitions of the other concepts will be needed as well.

Operationalizing concepts for policy research can be riddled with difficulties. A policy concept may not be directly measurable within the time constraints of your study. For example, improvements in standardized test scores may take years to show up. If you have only a few months to show that an intervention improves school performance, you will need a different measure that can reliably indicate improvements (if they occur!) within a shorter period of time.

Policy concepts may be difficult to operationalize because they can't be directly observed. For example, the concept of *racial tolerance* is inferred from what people say and do. But if you ask them directly about their racial tolerance, people may not tell you what they really feel. Policy concepts that are politically sensitive are usually difficult to operationalize. People in a dictatorship may not want to admit to being oppressed for fear of reprisals. In some cases, different stakeholder groups may prefer alternative measures of a concept. For example, the U.S. government measures poverty among the elderly in terms of actual earned income, whereas some advocacy groups add the value of government benefits to actual earned income to arrive at an assessment of poverty among the elderly. Still others may include physical and mental health in measuring how well off older Americans are.

Using Multiple Indicators

Using multiple indicators is one way to reduce the difficulties in operationalizing policy concepts. For example, if you are interested in interventions to improve the effectiveness of mental health centers, a single measure is unlikely to capture the many dimensions of center effectiveness. Therefore, you might decide to measure center effectiveness with a suite of metrics including improvement in patients' mental health, patient satisfaction, employee morale, community support for the center, partnerships with local support and employment services, and the cost-efficiency of service delivery. While different stakeholders may prefer different indicators, using a suite of indicators is likely to satisfy the needs of most stakeholders. If you combine these multiple indicators into an index of effectiveness, be sure to explain exactly how you arrived at the final measure (e.g., Did you weight some indicators more than others? Did you add them or multiply them?)

An advantage of using multiple indicators of concepts is the ability to shed light on why a policy intervention works or doesn't. Remember the theory of the intervention (the "hoW?")? Interventions like the Head Start Program can work in different ways, for instance, by affecting physical health or self-confidence or the amount of support a child receives from parents. Knowing "hoW?" the intervention works in one setting is key to making sure it works in another setting. And one way to know this is by looking at the possibly differing effects of an intervention on multiple indicators. An intervention in mental health care centers may increase patient satisfaction with treatment but not reduce the length of treatment or the cost of care. Information like this can provide invaluable guidance to policy makers. Using multiple indicators is especially valuable for tracking possible negative side effects of interventions because, even if some indicators improve, others many actually get worse. And when multiple indicators point in the same positive direction, they can increase your confidence that the intervention really works.

Using Proxy and Unobtrusive Measures

When operationalizing policy concepts, you may find it helpful to adopt proxy and unobtrusive measures. Proxy measures are approximate, indirect assessments of a concept. Proxies are needed particularly when your concepts cannot be directly measured. For example, proxy indicators of a community's racial tolerance include unemployment rates among racial minorities, racial attitudes as reported in a survey of randomly selected citizens, hate crime statistics, the distribution of school funding, and the locations of retail stores in various parts of the community. None of these indicators provides an adequate assessment of a community's racial tolerance. Together, though, they at least give a sense of what life might be like for racial minorities who live there.

Unobtrusive measures allow you to assess the concept without the direct participation of stakeholders. Conducting a survey of patient or employee satisfaction is very obtrusive and runs the risk of influencing the results. ("You must care about me enough to ask, so I guess I'm satisfied." "I don't want to say anything that will hurt feelings or get someone in trouble.") Unobtrusive measures, on the other hand, don't require people to do anything out of the ordinary. Cost of care data (normally collected and reported for insurance reimbursement purposes anyway) is an example of an unobtrusive measure of hospital effectiveness. The incidence of hate crimes reported to police is a possible unobtrusive measure of a community's racial tolerance.

- Precisely define each key concept in your policy research question
- Avoid bias in measuring concepts
- Include multiple indicators of important concepts
- Include indicators of possible negative side effects
- Use proxy measures when concepts cannot be directly measured
- Use unobtrusive measures when measurement may affect the behavior

Table 4.2   Advice for Operationalizing Policy Concepts

Mixing unobtrusive and obtrusive indicators is often needed to measure a policy concept adequately, because one type of indicator compensates for the inadequacies of the other. Obtrusive measures are often more focused on the exact concept of interest, but unobtrusive measurement is less likely to change people's behavior. By including both, you can increase your confidence in the study's findings. Table 4.2 summarizes our recommendations for operationalizing concepts.

Activity 4.2 Decide Between Primary and Secondary Data Collection

After operationalizing your policy concepts, you are ready for the next big design decision: Will you collect and analyze evidence in existing data sources (secondary data collection)? Or will you collect and analyze entirely new evidence (primary data collection)?

Many policy researchers do not even consider new primary data collection. For some policy areas, many well-known data resources already exist, and mining them for answers to policy questions is a respected tradition. However, we believe that primary data collection has many advantages for policy research, and we encourage you to try it. In this section, we begin with secondary data collection because this is the more familiar policy research approach. Then, we explain the advantages of and answer some objections to doing primary research as a way to obtain new evidence on targeted research questions.

Secondary Data Collection

For many policy research questions, new evidence can be obtained by analyzing existing data archives. Data archives are collections of facts and information on a particular subject. For example, the U.S. Census Bureau makes available data about the U.S. population from 1902 to the present day. Among the data provided by the Census Bureau are birth and death rates by region; population density per state or region; ethnic and gender distribution by region, state, and county; life expectancy; infant mortality rates; and net migration rates.

Archives can be useful for answering a targeted research question about whether capital punishment deters crime, for example. You might compare crime statistics in states with capital punishment with crime statistics in states that outlaw it. You could find crime statistics in a year's Statistical Abstract for Law Enforcement (part of the U.S. Census Bureau archive). To learn which states permit capital punishment and which do not, you could go to a website like www.deathpenaltyinfo.org or look for resolutions by the United Nations Human Rights Committee. You could then perform a relatively straightforward statistical analysis of differences in crime data across the states to help form your policy recommendation.

Table 4.3 presents other examples of data archives available to policy researchers. Included in this list is a data archive with geospatial data, also referred to as geographical information system (GIS) data. GIS data are increasingly useful for policy research. GIS data come in the form of *shape* files, which indicate specific coordinates on the world map where each point of interest is located. Shape files can be overlaid on each other to identify patterns across different geographical regions.

For example, the Easter Island governing council wanted to encourage economic development for tourism with minimal damage to the island's many significant archeological artifacts. Island topological features, the geographical coordinates of each artifact on the island, and the proposed locations of tourist support facilities (e.g., hotels, sewers), were overlaid and compared. The council learned that the density of artifacts was often greatest in small valleys in which sewers were proposed. Consequently, the council adopted a new policy requiring developers to check the GIS overlay for artifacts; the policy saved countless artifacts from destruction.

Secondary data sources are popular with policy analysts for studies of the cost-effectiveness of particular interventions, a methodology we explain in more detail below. When the data available in the data archives match very closely with the concepts operationalized from the targeted question, the use of secondary data analysis is appropriate and effective. For example, a Stanford University graduate student in biomedical informatics reanalyzed data in the U.S. Food and Drug Administration's archives and learned that a set of drugs widely prescribed for high cholesterol and depression had adverse health effects (McBride, 2011).

At the same time, it's important to recognize that the facts in archives were collected and assembled by people for purposes different from yours.

Title	Website	Description
CIA World Factbook	www.cia.gov/library/ publications/the-world-factbook/	Offers data about different aspects of every nation including geography, literacy rates, annual gross domestic products, and birth and death rates
The World Bank Data	http://data.worldbank .org/	Provides up-to-date data on topics such as aid effectiveness, social development, labor, and social protection
Gallup	www.gallup.com/	Publishes polls on different aspects of political life, such as employment rates, presidential approval, and military issues
Association of Religion Data Archives	www.thearda .com/Archive/browse .asp	Presents data about the domestic and international distribution of people by religious affiliation
State Department	www.state.gov/	Maintains statistics about countries, including human trafficking and the arms trade and details of past actions taken on those issues
Bureau of Labor Statistics	www.bls.gov/	Reports domestic and international employment and productivity statistics
Department of Commerce	www.commerce .gov/news/fact-sheets	Gives fact sheets on many areas of economic activity, such as manufacturing of additives, digital literacy, and exports
American National Election Studies	www.electionstudies .org/	Provides data from interview-based surveys of people in most national election years since 1948
General Social Survey	www3.norc.org/ gss+website/	Contains a standard core of answers to demographic, behavioral, and attitudinal questions since 1972, plus topics of special interest

(Continued)

(Continued)

Title	Website	Description
Inter-university Consortium for Political and Social Research data archive	www.icpsr.umich.edu	Provides raw data from surveys, censuses, and administrative records originally gathered by partners such as Health and Medical Care Archive, National Archive of Computerized Data on Aging, National Archive of Criminal Justice Data, Substance Abuse and Mental Health Data Archive, and Child Care & Early Education Research Connections
U.S. government geospatial data	geo.data.gov	Provides web-based access to maps, government data, and geospatial services including more than 400,000 (primarily geospatial) datasets from 172 agencies across the U.S. federal government

Table 4.3   Example Data Archives for Policy Research

The measures in them may conform poorly to your definitions of important policy concepts, and changes in the way measurements were made over time are often difficult for the users of archives to assess. The data may be too old for confident extrapolation into the future. Therefore, we recommend against overreliance on secondary data sources and encourage you to pursue primary data collection when appropriate. Next, we discuss the advantages of primary data collection and respond to some objections about the time and expense required to do it.

Primary Data Collection

Consider a situation in which secondary data sources may not be a good fit for your targeted research question. Suppose you are interested in whether to recommend continuation of a set of agricultural practices that have been used for some years. Your analysis of secondary data found that use of those practices led to higher crop yields over the last 10 years than yields obtained with different practices. Are you justified in inferring that crop yields with those practices will remain high into the future? Probably not, when you consider possible changes in climate and consumer demand. Suppose you believe that countries in which large numbers of people don't pay the taxes they owe are more vulnerable to economic instability than countries with higher levels of compliance with tax laws. How well do you think that existing data archives, which publish data on taxes paid, will help you estimate nonpayment of taxes? How would you account for the people who didn't pay tax because they didn't owe tax? How would you figure out whether deductions claimed were or were not legitimate?

The point is that, although secondary data collection and analysis may be the most typical approach for obtaining new evidence on policy questions, it is not always the best approach. Primary data collection can be tailored much more carefully to specific unknowns, and fewer compromises are necessary in the measurement of concepts in primary than in secondary research.

Secondary data analysis is commonly thought to be cheaper and faster than primary research. That is no longer always the case. Data can be collected over the Internet, and there are inexpensive crowdsourcing options such as Mechanical Turk (from Amazon) to help with data collection and analysis. Even when secondary data analysis is in fact cheaper and faster, you need to weigh the cost and speed of research against the risks of a bad decision arising from inappropriate measures. Getting creative about how you collect new evidence often provides far more insight into the problem than accepting the limitations of secondary data analysis. You might be able to reframe your targeted research question in ways that yield important insights for policy formulation. If, for example, you change the question from "How many people in this country don't pay the taxes they owe?" to "Where in this country are the greatest opportunities for tax evasion?" you may find that that primary data collection is fast and cheap and provides great ideas about needed policy change.

We are often asked the following: "How can I gather new primary evidence? I'm just [a student, a civil servant, or staff member working alone, someone with little time or resources—pick one]." However, in our experience, the biggest barrier to new primary research is not time, experience, or money, but the wrong mind-set. A mind-set conducive to gathering new evidence is one we call the *LOFE mind-set:* leverage, optimism, focus, and enthusiasm. *Leverage* refers to making use of other people's resources, not just your own. We often have been able to convince organizations to set up field experiments to help answer our policy research questions because they too had been wondering how to deliver their services more effectively. *Optimism* means not giving up easily when your early attempts to leverage others' resources fail. In

one policy research study, we had to ask more than 100 companies to participate in order to get 15 to say yes. *Focus* means taking one step in the policy
research journey at a time. Don't worry in the Obtain New Evidence Phase
about what you did back in the Synthesize Existing Evidence Phase or what
you will need to do during the Design Policy Recommendations Phase. Focus
now on designing a meaningful and manageable search for new evidence.
Enthusiasm means the energy you communicate to others. When we are enthu-
siastic about data gathering, we often find others volunteering to join us. We
encourage you to develop a LOFE attitude toward primary policy research.

Activity 4.3 Choose a Data Collection Method

Many methods can be used to obtain new evidence. Here, we describe five
methods particularly suitable for policy research: (1) cost-benefit and its vari-
ants cost-effectiveness and social impact assessments, (2) field experiments,
(3) interviews, (4) surveys, and (5) case studies. For each method, we include
an example of a policy research study that used this method.

Cost-Benefit, Cost-Effectiveness, and Social Impact Assessments

Cost-benefit analysis is a set of methods in which a researcher compares the
costs and benefits of alternative policy options, including doing nothing. For
example, cost-benefit analyses of a tax incentive for private health insurance
might compare the costs and benefits of different levels of insurance and different tax incentives. In its purest form, cost-benefit analysis attributes a monetary value to the benefits of a policy option and compares them with the costs,
again measured in dollars. By using a common yardstick for both costs and
benefits, the relative attractiveness of alternatives can be readily determined.

The Federal Highway Administration (FHWA)—a branch of the U.S.
Department of Transportation—uses cost-benefit analyses of operating costs,
safety costs, and time when comparing alternative transportation networks. By
converting safety and time concerns into monetary values, FHWA makes decisions about improvements in the U.S. highway system (Federal Highway
Administration, 2011). Similarly, the costs of dam construction and maintenance projects can be calculated in monetary terms and compared to the dollar
value of benefits like hydroelectric power and water for agriculture. To decide
which of several alternative water resource projects to undertake, a government agency could rank them according to their benefit-to-cost ratios and
select the most beneficial ones.

A major drawback of the cost-benefit analysis approach in policy
research is the difficulty of assigning money values to the costs of

outcomes such as death, suffering, and social unrest and to benefits such as reduced child abuse, fair housing practices, and better schools. Pure cost-benefit analyses seem most appropriate for infrastructure projects in which the risks of severe negative side effects (e.g., dam failure, pollution of ground water, birth defects) are relatively low. Not only is it difficult to value the costs and benefits of many policy changes in money, these analyses do not really account for uneven distribution of costs and benefits across stakeholder groups (Munger, 2000). Even if the benefits of a dam outweigh its costs in monetary terms, what does it mean if all the benefits go to wealthy agricultural companies and all the costs of the project are borne by poor people who are forced to move from their land? Who actually compensates them? And does compensation in money really balance their losses?

Variations on the cost-benefit analysis approach have been developed to address some of its limitations. One variation is cost-effectiveness analysis. In cost-effectiveness analysis, the benefits are expressed not in monetary terms but in terms of the achievement of certain outcomes. Costs are still quantified in dollars. So in a cost-effectiveness analysis of alcohol abuse treatments, a policy researcher might compute and compare the costs of turning around one alcohol abuser in each of several treatment programs in order to select the most cost-effective program.

Dwyer (2006) used secondary data to analyze the costs and effects of legislation that had raised water prices for everyone in Australia in an effort to

Costs (of current restrictions)	*Benefits (in changing restrictions)*
• Generally increased water prices unfair to citizens • Complex regulations used to cap urban water use (such as time constraints for sprinkler systems) inconvenience people • Environmental degradation • Halting of dam construction, cutting off employment opportunities for some	• Fairer distribution of water pricing based on actual water use as opposed to scarcity of water in area • More flexible policy decisions in each region as opposed to blanket restrictions for the country as a whole • Greater responsiveness to actual level of "scarcity" of water • Increase in land value • Slight increase in employment from decision not to halt dam construction

Table 4.4   Cost-Effectiveness Analysis Example

(Adapted from Dwyer, 2006)

move more of the water supply into urban areas. The costs of the policy were found to be negative environmental impacts, lower land values due to environmental degradation, and water prices that did not reflect the true costs of alternative water uses. The analysis, summarized in Table 4.4, led to the conclusion that a change in policy would yield significant benefits for most stakeholder groups.

Another alternative to cost-benefit analysis is social impact assessment. Cost-effectiveness analyses, like their cost-analysis brethren, may too easily emphasize economic costs and benefits, ignoring the other STORM context conditions. Policy researchers use social impact assessments to evaluate not just economic impacts but also impacts on people, social relationships, and organizations. For example, a social impact assessment of a proposed new highway should examine how construction would affect the aesthetics of the neighborhood and the social interaction patterns of residents in addition to the commute times of through commuters. In Boston, the multibillion-dollar, decade-long Big Dig project was undertaken to try to reverse the damage done to urban aesthetics and community experience by an elevated highway constructed primarily with commuters in mind.

The cost-benefit plus cost-effectiveness plus social impact analysis category of methods is the set of approaches most frequently used in policy research. But this does not need to be the case as other research designs, mentioned briefly next, are often high-quality alternatives. Furthermore, although most policy research using these methods analyzes secondary data, this is also an unnecessary restriction. If this category of methods suits your problem, don't limit yourself to what you can find in databases. Why not call social service agencies directly to identify areas in which their costs are currently escalating? Why not ask businesses directly about the benefits they get from installing pollution-abatement equipment?

Field Experiments

A highly beneficial alternative to the cost-benefit family of approaches to collecting data on policy problems is the field experiment. In a field experiment, policy researchers in cooperation with stakeholder partners actually implement an intervention designed to solve a policy problem in a real-life setting. The outcomes of the intervention are then tracked over a period of time. Because the intervention is actually tried (or *piloted* as in a *pilot project*) in the kind of setting it was intended for, field experiments provide invaluable data for policy researchers that no amount of secondary data analysis can replicate.

Like laboratory experiments, some field experiments employ random assignment of subjects to treatment conditions and control groups. The advantage of this strategy is increased confidence that the treatment caused the outcomes observed. However, field experiments have very different dynamics from the typical, university-based lab experiment with undergraduate student subjects. If you're an unfortunate victim of Lou Gehrig's disease, you do not want to participate in a clinical trial where you may be assigned to the *placebo group* (a control group that gets a treatment known to be ineffective); you want to be one of the people who receive a promising, new treatment. In certain situations, attempting to assign people to experimental treatments randomly may actually violate research ethics.

Not surprisingly, most field experiments do not employ random assignment and control groups and, for that reason, are often called *quasi-experiments* (Shadish, Cook, & Campbell, 2002). These approaches do not have the kind of experimental control that convinces scientists beyond a doubt about the effectiveness of an intervention. But, for policy researchers, they are almost the Holy Grail because they produce information that is utterly convincing to participants and many other stakeholders.

Consider the example of two educational interventions. If students get to choose which classroom they'll attend (nonrandomized assignment) and their test scores improve, researchers may question whether self-selection and the placebo effect (the belief that the treatment will lead to improvement induces people to improve) explain the findings. But when full experimental control is not possible, policy researchers can do only their best to match classrooms (in terms of students' age, gender, average intelligence, and truancy rates, etc.) that receive the "treatment" with those who do not (the control group) and observe what happens. If you take enough care with how you match and compare the experimental and nonexperimental conditions, you may produce evidence that really answers your questions and persuades decision makers.

One of us (Ann) designed a randomized field experiment for the U.S. armed forces at a time when unauthorized absence (i.e., the recruit did not show up for morning roll call) was a problem. The Army found that punishing recruits didn't decrease the absences. But unauthorized absence is a real problem for military discipline. (Imagine a troop transport ready to take off: "Where's Smith?") Interviews with some commanders and recruits, followed by broader-reaching questionnaire surveys, showed that most unauthorized absences were for family emergencies (sick children, parent–teacher conferences) rather than an indication that recruits were going absent without leave (AWOL), which is usually interpreted as an indication that a soldier has defected, a condition that in wartime is punishable by death.

After much discussion, military leaders agreed to try a field experiment. The experimental intervention changed how the recruit's unauthorized absence was handled by the recruit's commanding officers. Officers were trained to instruct recruits to communicate immediately in the case of unavoidable absence and to provide contact information (e.g., cell phone number) in case the unit was deployed and the recruit needed to report instantly. If a recruit's absences became too frequent, officers were encouraged to provide counseling.

In the field experiment, officers in one half of the units were trained in the new way to handle unauthorized absences. Over the course of 6 months, unauthorized absences were tracked in all units. And at the end of that period, recruits (who had not received any training—only their officers had) were asked to report on changes in officers' behavior. In units where officers were conscientiously trained in new behaviors, unauthorized absences went down significantly. The responses by recruits in those units verified that changes in officers' behavior made a difference in recruits' behavior. Table 4.5 summarizes this field experiment.

Interviews

Another method for gathering primary data to address your targeted question is through interviews. Interviewing is a strategy for collecting information by asking people directly, usually in person or by telephone. Because interviews are interactive conversations, they allow you to confirm your understanding of what people tell you on the spot. In many situations, policy researchers have the added goal of building relationships with people during interviews in order to leverage their resources and support.

Good interviewing is an art. Interviewers have to help respondents become comfortable enough to share their knowledge and experiences. Interviewers have to make adjustments in the questions they ask to understand and respond effectively to what respondents tell them.

"Why?" (Intended Outcomes of the Intervention) and "Who and Where?" (Context)	Reduce unauthorized absences of military personnel on base in the United States
"What?" (Nature of Intervention)	Instructions to be followed by officers in the case of unauthorized absences by recruits
Results Observed	Military recruits in experimental units were less likely to take unauthorized absences than recruits in the control units

Table 4.5   Field Experiment to Reduce Unauthorized Absences in the U.S. Military

Interview questions can be closed-ended or open-ended. Closed-ended questions are ones that request a straightforward answer like "yes," "all the time," or "10." Examples include "When did you start participating in this program?" or "How often do your clients report problems with the intervention?" Open-ended questions are broad, conversational questions that request the interviewee to discuss a situation in some detail. Examples include "Tell me about your experiences with this program" and "What happened when you tried the intervention?" Asking open-ended questions is especially good to do when you want to increase your understanding of a situation or develop your relationship with the person you interview. In a typical interview, you will find yourself combining questions of both types, using open-ended questions to encourage the interviewee to talk and to probe answers and closed-ended questions to confirm specific details of interest to you. Of course, when you have only a few minutes of someone's time, asking a short list of structured, closed-ended questions may be the best approach.

It is important to tailor interview questions to the knowledge of those you interview. If you have a long list of questions about, say, companies' health care insurance benefits for employees, you should divide the questions into topics that fit the expertise of different kinds of respondents. For instance, human resource management specialists are the best people to tell you about the kinds of coverage offered, the reasons for offering that coverage, and its cost to the company. Supervisors may be the best people to tell you about the benefits of offering health care insurance coverage to potential new employees. Employees are the best people to tell you how health care insurance affects their commitment to their employer and their satisfaction at work.

Policy researchers need to take pains to assess the reliability of interview data. One employee's experiences may not be representative of others, so you will need a strategy for selecting different kinds of employees to talk with and deciding how many employees to talk to. Similarly, what the human resources specialist tells you in an interview about the company's total health care costs may not be an accurate recollection. So a plan for collecting backup documents is often be a good idea.

Surveys

Surveys also collect information directly from people by asking them questions. But surveys are typically more formal and structured than interviews. The questions in a survey are carefully worded, written down, and closed-ended in form. The survey is then distributed to respondents by mail, e-mail, or the web, and the researcher may not be present when the recipient completes the survey.

The noninteractive nature of the survey strategy usually does not allow respondents to ask the researchers questions if respondents don't understand a survey question. And researchers cannot ask respondents what they mean if they don't understand a respondent's answer. Therefore, a great deal of effort is required up front to ensure that surveys produce reliable and valid information. There is a wealth of good advice for designing effective surveys, covering everything from selecting a representative sample of respondents, wording questions, how to avoid response bias, where to place questions on a page or a screen, and how to attract and retain respondent motivation to complete the survey. You should definitely follow this good advice!

The design of the survey depends on the targeted question. For example, for a policy research problem about pumps for irrigation in Central Africa, you may have a targeted question such as this: "Which pumps work best for the longest time with little maintenance under extremely sandy conditions?" To answer this question, you might survey manufacturers about customer feedback on different types of pumps, villagers about their experiences using different types of pumps, or even farmers elsewhere in the world who work in sandy soil. You may administer the manufacturers' survey of closed-ended questions online, ask the villagers open-ended questions in face-to-face settings, and ask the farmers in other countries to fill out paper-and-pencil forms and return them by mail. Textbox 4.1 shows an example of a survey-based policy research study.

Textbox 4.1: Example Policy Research Survey Study

Dr. Michael Klein surveyed women in British Colombia to learn how they had prepared themselves for childbirth. Fewer than 30 percent of the 1,318 respondents had attended prenatal childbirth classes (Roan, 2011). The others had used books or the Internet to gain knowledge. Sadly, however, most of those who had not attended classes could not answer basic questions about the benefits, drawbacks, and safety concerns of common childbirth medical procedures such as epidurals or Cesarean surgery.

Case Studies

The case study is a research strategy in which the researcher attempts to gain deep knowledge about how an individual (or a village, company, etc.) functions in that individual's normal context (a family, a care center, a job, etc.). The case study researcher typically uses a variety of data-gathering approaches to study the individual, including interviews, observations, unobtrusive measures, and analysis of documents. The case study approach is particularly good for answering questions about how people do things and why they do them as they do. The case study approach is also valuable when researchers believe that STORM context conditions (e.g., sandy soil, threat of layoffs, urban violence) are very important but do not know exactly how they influence the individual.

Unlike in surveys, where respondents are often selected randomly, the individuals selected for case studies are carefully chosen to fill in particular gaps in the researcher's knowledge. For example, they may be selected because they achieved particularly good outcomes (or particularly bad ones) from an intervention, because they have developed an innovative solution to a problem, or because they are experiencing major challenges in trying to implement an intervention. The case study researcher looks for information that provides richness of detail about the context; for unexpected relationships between factors, people, or events; and for a generally deeper understanding of the phenomenon.

For example, a case study of how forests recover from devastating fires might focus on how returning insects, birds, animals, and plant life affect each other. Case studies are very hard to do well. Some policy researchers conduct a few interviews and call their research a case study. This is not accurate. Case studies examine many aspects of a single case in depth using a variety of data sources. Case study researchers often have the problems of too much data and difficulty analyzing it for patterns. Because many case studies examine individuals over some period of time, the challenge of finding patterns is particularly acute.

Textbox 4.2 gives an example of policy research using the case study method.

Textbox 4.2: Example of Case Study–Based Policy Research

This case study examined the crack-cocaine industry in East Harlem, New York ("El Barrio"; Bourgois, 2002). The focal point of the study was a particular dealer, called Ray, and his employees as they interacted with customers at a vending point called The Game Room. The anthropologist who conducted the study used his personal experiences of living in El Barrio, crack dealers' stories of failed hopes and dreams, and quantitative data from a variety of sources to paint a rich picture of poverty in the area and the challenges people face in trying to escape it. From this evidence, the researcher drew policy recommendations that included destroying the profitability of the cocaine industry by decriminalization coupled with an aggressive approach to creating job opportunities in the inner city.

Which Method to Use?

Each policy research approach has strengths and weaknesses and is better suited to certain research purposes, as summarized in Table 4.6. Consequently, policy researchers will often design studies using multiple methods to leverage advantages and overcome weaknesses. For example, they might conduct an in-depth case study of many aspects of a single local health clinic, followed by a survey of all health clinics in the region about a few important issues. Base your research design decisions on your targeted research question, but use your creativity to obtain the best possible new evidence within your resource constraints!

Activity 4.4 Confront Ethical Concerns

Ethical issues arise in policy research because research can result in unintended harm to the people studied. Several U.S. government agencies publish guidelines for the protection of human subjects in research (e.g., www .hhs.gov/ohrp). These guidelines include giving people choices about participating and guaranteeing the confidentiality of information collected. If you're employed by a university when you do policy research, you will be required to submit your research plans to your university's Institutional Review Board (IRB) for oversight. IRBs comprise faculty and staff members who have been trained on guidelines for human subject protection.

Policy researchers often face ethical dilemmas that are not clearly covered by such guidelines (Nagel, 1984). The dilemmas include how to avoiding taking sides, how to ensure equitable treatment of stakeholders, when and with whom to share preliminary research results, and so forth. Based on our observations of policy research studies (our own and others'), we propose a minimal set of ethical standards for you. Feel free to add to them as your experience grows.

Never Change Your Data

The data are what the data are. Even if you "know" that the person filling out the survey "didn't mean what she said," or that the manager in the case study doesn't normally yell at employees, you are ethically bound to report what you see. You may give a justification for ignoring certain observations, but you should report them first.

Avoid Collecting and Storing Identity Information

Policy researchers often need ways to identify respondents uniquely. They need to be able, for example, to link interview transcripts to a person's survey data or outcome scores. It is tempting to use government-issued identifiers,

	Data Archives	Cost-Effectiveness/Social Impact Assessment	Field Experiments	Interviews and Surveys	Case Studies
Strengths	Analysis can be inexpensive and quick because data are already assembled by others	Allows alternative interventions to be compared on the same yardstick	Allows for direct observation of an intervention implemented in context; helps to establish that an intervention produces particular outcomes	Opportunity to explore issues and build relationships (interviews); relatively inexpensive primary data collection if Internet based (e.g., surveys)	Examines individuals in context; in-depth understanding; good for exploring unintended consequences of interventions
Weaknesses	Measures may not capture policy research concepts well	Requires converting costs and benefits to comparable units (usually money), which is not always easy or appropriate	Full experimental control (random assignment of subjects to treatments) is rarely possible; requires extensive participation and effort on the part of stakeholders	More costly and time-consuming than secondary analysis (both); unstructured data analysis (interviews)	Unstructured data collection and analysis; potential loss of research focus
Best Suited For	Identifying incidence and magnitude of policy problems; providing data for cost-effectiveness studies	Comparing alternative interventions that have relatively low risks and relatively equitable distributions of costs and risks across stakeholders	Situations in which the applicability and effectiveness of particular interventions are unknown	Studying problems and interventions about which secondary data are lacking	Exploring the effects of context on the problem; showing how and why interventions work when they do

Table 4.6 Comparison of Policy Research Methods

such as social security numbers, passport numbers, and employee identification numbers. Do not use them! Private, unique identifiers are often used for access to confidential records and financial accounts. If you collect these identifiers, and they are lost or stolen (such as by a computer hacker), you will be required by law to report the loss and notify the victims. You may even be subject to prosecution.

So instead of using private, unique identifiers, make up your own. Then, destroy the information by which people can be identified, such as name, e-mail address, or employer. This way, you can limit the chances of unintentional harm to the people you studied. For example, if you collect data about how satisfied employees are at work, an employer may want to identify dissatisfied people and take action against them. If you only knew identifier codes and not people's identities, you wouldn't be able to provide the information, even if you wanted to.

Tell Participants the Study's Results, and Let Them Comment

When people participate in a study, they know that you are conducting the study to learn something. Therefore, it is important for you to tell them what you have learned and let them tell you whether your results fit their experiences and are reported and interpreted accurately. If they agree with your conclusions, it can increase your confidence in your policy recommendations. If they find factual errors, you should correct them. If they disagree with your interpretations of the facts, it may encourage you to learn more.

Never Overpromise the Impacts of Your Research

In order to motivate people to participate in studies, researchers sometimes make statements like this: "These data will be used in making decisions about what services you will be provided." The problem with these promises is that you cannot keep them—only policy makers can do this. All you can do is to provide the findings and recommendations to policy makers; you cannot guarantee that they will be used. By not promising too much, you won't create unmet expectations.

Don't Waste Respondents' Time

U.S. federal guidelines clearly state that research should never harm people, even unintentionally. For example, if you start an intervention to curb childhood obesity and learn that a child has been punished at home for not following the instructions, you should end the intervention immediately. That's a clear instance of harm. A less obvious, but still important harm, in our view, is wasting respondents' time.

Policy researchers should avoid asking the same question twice. They should listen well and take notes the first time so that respondents don't have to go over the same ground again. The purpose of policy research is to deliver value to stakeholders, including research participants. Respecting their time is one way to deliver value.

Our minimal list of ethical guidelines is summarized in Table 4.7.

Activity 4.5 Assess Your Needs for Confidence in the Evidence

Each method (cost-benefit or effectiveness assessments, field experiments, interviews, surveys, and case studies) has the potential to provide valuable answers to your targeted question. However, no method gives you perfect data. There are always errors in data: Maybe the cost information you used for your cost-effectiveness study was too old; possibly the metrics of intervention success you used in a field experiment were too narrow; perhaps managers were distracted by planned layoffs when you interviewed them; perhaps survey respondents did not read the questions carefully; maybe the "effective" agency you selected for your case study was not at all similar to your target agency.

Therefore, throughout your data collection effort, you should assess your confidence in the data and ask whether it's sufficient for the conclusions you want to draw. If your confidence is low, you may want to redesign your data collection method. What kind of situation would make you want to do this? Suppose you planned to ask the village leader for permission to interview people about the effectiveness of the irrigation pumps they use. If you find out that the village head is a relative of the pump supplier, you may start to suspect that villagers will not be candid with you about problems with the pump. That is, data you obtain by asking people directly are likely to be biased, and you'll need some other way to get accurate data. Problems like these are rarely insurmountable, but you do have to be on your guard

- Never change your data
- Avoid collecting and storing identity information
- Tell participants the study's results, and let them comment
- Never overpromise the impacts of your research
- Don't waste respondents' time

Table 4.7 Ethical Guidelines for Policy Researchers

against situations that could significantly reduce your confidence in policy recommendations you base on the evidence.

The simple rule is that, the more confidence you need in the evidence—for instance, when the costs are great and catastrophic risks can be envisioned—the more care you should take in obtaining new evidence. You can increase your confidence when you design evidence collection by repeatedly asking yourself this question: "What other explanation could there be for data that suggest [improved outcomes, no change in outcomes, bad outcomes]?" The most creative part of evidence collection design lies in generating "plausible alternative explanations" (Shadish et al., 2002) that give insight into the validity (or lack of validity) of your evidence. For example, findings that an intervention did not have the desired effect could mean that the intervention was bad or that it was poorly implemented (villagers weren't trained to use the new pumps; spare parts had not been delivered, etc.). Unless you can rule out the possibility that the intervention was badly implemented, you can't validly conclude on the basis of your evidence that the intervention didn't work. (How could you rule out the threat to the validity of your evidence about irrigation pump effectiveness posed by the village leader's family connection with the pump supplier?)

Designing studies in ways that eliminate plausible alternative hypotheses is a creative process. Experts such as your advisers can help you. And you can work with a small number of your study participants or stakeholders to conduct a pilot implementation of proposed interventions. Show your research design and expected results to your experts and the members of your pilot group; ask them to come up with plausible alternative explanations for your expected results; and then think up ways to rule out those alternatives. (For example, you could talk to people in other villages who are using the same pump.)

Coming up with persuasive answers to the most plausible alternative hypotheses about your findings and ruling the hypotheses out can add significantly to the time and cost of policy research. Therefore, you should estimate how much confidence you need for the recommendations you'll want to make. You need lower confidence to recommend a field experiment or pilot project of a simple, low-risk, easily reversible intervention than you would need to recommend a full-scale implementation of a costly and risky infrastructure project.

OBTAIN NEW EVIDENCE PHASE DELIVERABLES

The first deliverable of the Obtain New Evidence Phase is an evidence collection design memo. The final deliverable is a report summarizing the findings you (or someone else) obtained after executing your research design.

Deliverable 4.1 New Evidence Collection Design Memo

Having completed the five activities discussed earlier, you should document your research design choices in a design memo. The design memo describes the nature of the evidence you want to obtain, how the evidence will be collected, and how much confidence you need in the collected evidence. The design memo will be short (two to four pages), including the following topics:

The Targeted Research Question. Briefly explain why obtaining additional evidence is needed. Summarize what is not known about the policy problem and its solution and how the targeted research question addresses knowledge gaps. For example, you might note that two solutions have been proposed for a problem, but no evidence exists about their costs, benefits, and risks.

The Target Population. Identify the stakeholder group about whom evidence will be obtained: those who experience the policy problem (e.g., the homeless, the hungry, cancer patients, poor women in India), those who provide relevant services (e.g., clinics, banks, caregivers), or some other group. Describe the ethical and practical issues involved in collecting evidence from or about this target population. For example, does the evidence need to be collected orally, by observation, through a translator, only with permission of a leader, and so on? What safeguards need to be put in place to ensure confidentiality?

The Evidence to Be Obtained. Describe the data to be collected. Here, you provide definitions and operationalizations of key concepts, and you include precise instructions for conducting the intervention (if applicable). Be sure to include indicators of what is referred to as *treatment fidelity,* an assessment of how well the treatment was implemented compared to what you wanted. Asking soldiers to describe any changes observed in their officers' behavior gave an indication of treatment fidelity in the field experiment described earlier in this chapter.

The Evidence Collection Method. Explain how you want the evidence to be collected. If your design involves a case study of an organization, how many of what kind of people should be interviewed and over what time period? What documents should be collected? How will the data be summarized and presented? Also, in this section, you would explain how you want the evidence gathering to be wrapped up. For instance, you might specify debriefing meetings for study participants and the distribution of reports that summarize study findings.

How Confidence in the Evidence Will Be Ensured. In this section, you list the most plausible alternative hypotheses and describe how you plan to rule them out or the steps you expect someone else to take to instill confidence in the results.

After preparing the memo, solicit comments from your advisers, and add them to your memo! If need be, make changes to your design to address their

comments. Table 4.8 gives an example of Deliverable 4.1 for the military field
experiment on unauthorized absences by recruits.

Targeted Research Question	Will a training program that instructs military commanders to treat unauthorized absences differently than previously reduce the unauthorized absence rate among recruits?
Target Population	Recruits' unauthorized absence behavior and commanders' use of the training instructions
Evidence to Be Obtained	Incidence of unauthorized absence by recruits; recruits' observations of changes in commanders' behavior
Evidence Collection Method	Implement the training program in randomly identified military units, leaving the remaining half of the units as a control condition; unauthorized absences will be tracked as normally done; survey recruits at the end of the intervention to indicate treatment fidelity
How Confidence in the Evidence Will Be Ensured	Random assignment; survey recruits about a variety of STORM context conditions to test for differences over time or between experimental and control groups
Advisers' Comments	Need to make sure that assignment of units to treatment condition is representative of unit size and geographic location

Table 4.8   Example of Deliverable 4.1 (New Evidence Collection Design Memo) for a Field Experiment

Policy Research Problem	How can unauthorized absences by recruits be reduced?
Targeted Question	Will a training program that instructs military commanders to treat unauthorized absences differently than previously reduce the unauthorized absence rate among recruits?
Design Decisions	Field experiment with random assignment of units to treatment
Differences Between Design and Actuality	Not all experimental units implemented all instructions; instead of comparing experimental units to control units, data analyses compared experimental units with high-treatment fidelity to all other units

Findings	The stronger the treatment fidelity, the higher the reduction in recruits' unauthorized absence
Confidence in Results	High because of random assignment and assessment of treatment fidelity

Table 4.9 Example of Deliverable 4.2 (Documented New Evidence) for a Field Experiment

Deliverable 4.2 Documented New Evidence

This deliverable should be another short memo, written after data collection has been carried out and findings have been analyzed. This short memo should follow the outline below:

1. Overall policy research problem summarized

2. Targeted policy research question

3. Summarized data collection design decisions (referring to Deliverable 4.1)

4. Differences (if any) between design decisions and the way data were really obtained

5. Findings from data analysis

6. Confidence in the results

See Table 4.9 for an example of Deliverable 4.2.

CONCLUSIONS

At the end of the Obtain New Evidence Phase, you have filled in gaps in your knowledge about the policy problem or its solution. You have confidence in the answers you obtained because you took care in operationalizing concepts, selecting a data-collection approach, and designing the data-collection effort in ways that ethically protected stakeholders and ruled out alternative hypotheses that could challenge your confidence in the evidence.

The decisions involved in obtaining new evidence are not easy to make. However, even new primary evidence collection is not something to be afraid of. For some of us, it is the most exciting aspect of policy research because there are no right answers, so much creativity is required, and you never quite know what will happen when the data collection starts, no matter how much time you spent in design. Be inspired, and have fun!

EXERCISES

1. Take two or three of the published research studies that you examined for the exercises in Chapter 3. For each one:
   - prepare a high-level outline of the major sections of the report
   - identify the method and the major study design choices made by the researchers
   - state the study's strengths and weaknesses, and compare them to the general pattern of strengths and weakness shown in Table 4.2
   - assess how much confidence you place in the findings

2. How would you design new primary evidence collection for each of the following targeted questions:
   - What interventions succeed in keeping homeless people off the streets?
   - What educational campaigns are most effective in mobilizing people to demand action on global climate change?
   - What infrastructure laws should be introduced to reduce the probability that tall buildings will collapse in the next 8.0 earthquake?
   - Does use of electronic health records reduce wait times in medical clinics?

5

Design Policy Recommendations

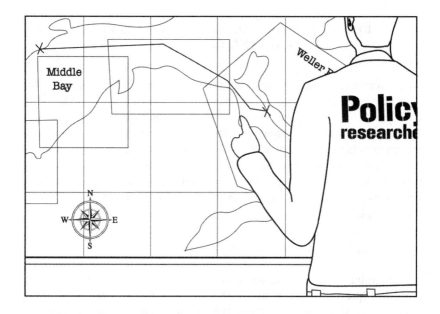

SUMMARY

Now that you are armed with evidence from your systematic review of exist-ing evidence (Chapter 3) and from any new evidence you generated (Chapter 4), you are in a position to design recommendations for your policy problem. The word *design* here indicates that making recommendations to policy makers is a highly creative process. Recommendations do not just fall out of your analysis mechanically; they have to be created—designed—from the analyses you have done with a dash of insight and deep connection to the policy problem. The Design Policy Recommendations Phase involves balancing the need to solve the policy problem with practical considerations such as timing, resource requirements, and political support. A key part of the Design Policy Recommendations Phase of the policy research process is coming up with a set of alternative interventions that is both meaningful—because only then will you make an improvement in the policy problem—and manageable—because having a manageable set of alternatives will help policy makers decide to take action. The four activities and the one major deliverable of the Design Policy Recommendations Phase are depicted in Figure 5.1.

DESIGN POLICY RECOMMENDATIONS PHASE TRACKING INDICATORS

After familiarizing yourself with the problem (Chapter 2), synthesizing the evidence (Chapter 3), and obtaining new evidence (Chapter 4), you probably think you have a good idea about the ideal solution to your policy problem. Are you done, then? Far from it! You haven't yet given policy makers the information they need in order to make an informed decision. The purpose of the Design Policy Recommendations Phase is to craft a decision document that lays out alternative courses of action and evaluates their pros and cons. Two (now familiar) tracking indicators will help you know that you have done this phase well.

Tracking Indicator 5.1 Meaningful Choices

The Design Policy Recommendations Phase is most successful when you are able to present policy makers with a meaningful and manageable choice among alternative courses of action. *Meaningful* means that the set of alternatives captures the range of most plausible opinions and evidence about what to do about the policy problem because this increases the chances that you will offer a solution that both is politically feasible and can actually improve the problem. Two points are important here. First, in the previous two chapters, we emphasized evidence—facts and data—particularly in the form of quantitative scientific research and disciplined, descriptive, observational accounts (e.g., case studies). Now, it's time to bring opinions back into the mix. The reason is that successful policy research requires confronting stakeholders' deeply held beliefs and preferences head-on. Acknowledging differing opinions, even if you don't agree with them, and evaluating them fairly support constructive dialogue and informed decision making. It also helps you build what we will refer to in Chapter 6 as a persuasive case for change.

Second, *meaningful* means that the alternatives you present to decision makers are all doable courses of action. Good policy recommendations are statements of what a policy maker (or the constituency she or he represents)

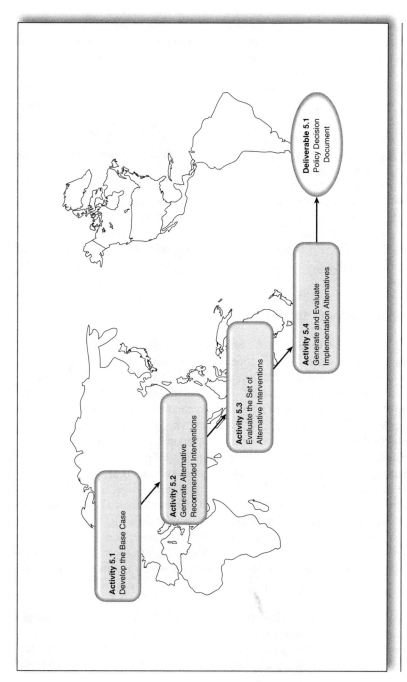

Figure 5.1 The Design Policy Recommendations Phase Voyage Map

should or should not do. Grammatically, they are imperative statements with action verbs, like *repeal the law* or *build the canal* or *support the program* or *implement a pilot program*. *Don't pursue legislation on this issue* can also be a good recommendation. (Later, we explain why *do nothing* and *wait and see* are good recommendations that have roles in policy research.) But statements like *consider repealing the law* or *think about building a canal* are not good recommendations, and you should avoid them. Why? Because there is no accountability. With think-about recommendations, there is no way for you and others to know whether or not these activities have been accomplished.

Finally, *meaningful* means that the policy options should be appropriate for the policy problem, that is, they should address at least one core dimension (preferably more) of your theory of the intervention (the "hoW?" of the Policy Solution Change Wheel), policy problem, and relevant STORM context conditions. If your recommendations are not appropriate, even if they are accepted and implemented, they will not have a chance of actually solving the policy problem.

Tracking Indicator 5.2 Manageable Choice

Giving policy makers a manageable choice among alternative courses of action means that you have reduced the number of alternatives—and the criteria by which the alternatives can be evaluated—down to a handful that can be meaningfully understood, remembered, and compared. There is no magic number of recommendations, but a good rule of thumb is four or five alternatives. Think of manageable choice in terms of the recommender systems developed for many complex consumer products such as automobiles, electronics, or home mortgages. In many product categories, there are literally hundreds of alternatives. If only one product attribute (e.g., color) is important to you, it may be quick and easy to run through a list of options to find the few relevant products. But what if your criteria include color, size, and price? Then, your decision problem is much more difficult. That's why good product-recommender systems allow you to compare, side by side, a small number of products that meet your criteria (e.g., *yellow, four inches or smaller, under $250*). Four or five alternatives can be manageably compared side by side, but 20 or 30 are far too many for a decision maker to handle well.

Both the number of alternatives and the number of criteria need to be manageable, but both the alternatives and the criteria need to be meaningful too. That means that they should address the policy problem and not leave out the interventions and criteria that are important to key stakeholders. If you leave out the interventions or criteria important to key stakeholders, they are likely to dismiss your analysis as biased or flawed. This is a challenging balancing act. That's why we use the word *design* to label this phase. Making good policy recommendations is a very creative activity. You can't do it well just by crunching numbers. You'll have to put on your thinking cap—and call on your advisers to challenge your ideas. This chapter offers a variety of suggestions and examples to guide you in the process of designing good policy recommendations.

DESIGN POLICY RECOMMENDATIONS PHASE ACTIVITIES

The Design Policy Recommendations Phase has four activities:

Activity 5.1: Develop the Base Case

Activity 5.2: Generate Alternative Recommended Interventions

Activity 5.3: Evaluate the Set of Alternative Interventions

Activity 5.4: Generate and Evaluate Implementation Alternatives

The first of the four activities in the Design Policy Recommendations Phase is to document the current situation in a way that makes clear the costs of doing nothing and clearly specifies the criteria against which different interventions (alternatives to doing nothing) can be evaluated. We call this the *Base Case.*

In the next two activities, you generate and evaluate alternative interventions aimed at changing the current situation. Once you get that far, your policy makers may decide to focus on a single, preferred course of action. Then, your task may shift to the fourth activity: generating and evaluating alternative ways to implement that preferred course of action.

For instance, let's suppose you've generated and evaluated two alternative ways to deal with corporate financial misconduct: (1) voluntary action and (2) tough, new regulations. Once your policy makers decide to pursue tough, new regulations, they may ask you to generate and evaluate alternative ways to implement those regulations. One implementation alternative might be to apply the regulations only to banks; another might be to apply them to all financial services providers, not just banks. Another set of implementation alternatives might be introducing the new regulations all at once versus phasing them in over a period of years.

Activity 5.1 Develop the Base Case

The Base Case is a description of the current situation presented in a way that spells out the costs of doing nothing and the criteria against which alternative courses of action should be evaluated. Earlier, we said that *do nothing* and *wait and see* are always options in policy decision making. There are several reasons for this.

Why Doing Nothing Can Be a Good Recommendation

First, doing nothing is sometimes the best solution. Doing nothing can be the best solution because introducing change always involves costs—whether in terms of money, time, lost opportunities (the benefits of doing something else), or possible risks. These costs sometimes outweigh both the disadvantages of the current situation and the benefits of the proposed solution. Suppose that digging a village well in Africa would increase crop yields by 5 percent but would also increase the cost of food by 10 percent (because the well has operating and maintenance costs). If people in the village are currently (just) managing to survive, the new "solution" could be a disaster.

Another cost that can make doing nothing an appropriate solution is the unintended negative consequences that may result from any intervention. For example, some university students designed a simple and inexpensive metal band that tripled the life of *mitads,* clay disks that Ethiopian villagers cook bread on. You might think this innovation was better than sliced bread. But, while benefiting many, the innovation threatened the livelihood of the people who make the clay disks (Beiser, 2011). (Licensing the mitad makers to sell the bands along with the mitads helped to reduce this problem. Later, we discuss how you may be able to anticipate unintended negative consequences and address them in your policy recommendations.)

Doing nothing (at least for now) can also be an appropriate recommendation when the extent of the problem or the effectiveness of the solution is highly uncertain. By waiting and carefully monitoring the situation, policy makers might be able to sense when the time is eventually right to pursue an intervention. Suppose you have symptoms that may or may not indicate a serious illness, and suppose the serious illness has a treatment that sometimes moderates the symptoms and sometimes causes nasty side effects (worse than the illness itself). Under conditions like these, most doctors would recommend that you come back next month for another checkup. The same is often true in many policy decisions.

Specifying the Base Case and Evaluation Criteria

Do nothing and *wait and see* are always policy alternatives. Sometimes, though, these options are not ideal because they allow the harms of the current situation to accumulate (e.g., global warming). Therefore, it is important for you to lay out the Base Case in a way that it makes clear to policy makers what the costs of doing nothing now really are. This means being explicit about who is being harmed, by how much, and in what way, using evidence you have assembled and analyzed. By documenting the Base Case (current situation), you are clearly articulating the nature (dimensions) and the extent (quantity) of the problem. The Base Case tells policy makers the cost of doing nothing about the problem. The Base Case also tells policy makers how much each alternative can be expected to improve each dimension of the problem at what cost, with what level of uncertainty, and with what potential negative side effects or risks. In other words, by developing the Base Case, you are articulating the criteria by which alternatives are to be evaluated.

The Policy Problem Change Wheel that you completed during the Launch Phase can simplify the activity of developing the Base Case. Important to generating the Base Case is identifying the dimensions along which the current situation should be evaluated: What kinds of harm are being done? Who gains while others lose? Where are the problems most acute? You should be sure to include issues that concern major groups of stakeholders who are likely to influence policy. For example, if your goal is to reduce teen pregnancies or sexually transmitted diseases, you are likely to consider a condom-distribution program as a possible intervention. Social conservatives often oppose such programs, arguing that they promote illicit sexual behavior. This means that the Base Case should include the dimension of sexual behavior norms and that you should assess the possibly of adverse effects on this dimension when you evaluate alternatives to the Base Case. Whatever dimensions you choose for describing the costs associated with the Base Case, use the same ones later when you evaluate alternative interventions.

The STORM context conditions you identified during the Launch Phase are often a good guide for generating dimensions for evaluating alternative recommended interventions. For instance, *cultural compatibility*—the fit between the intervention and what is familiar to key stakeholder groups—is an important dimension for evaluating many interventions. Other dimensions can be surfaced by thinking through the potential risks of an intervention. For example, some experts have argued that electronic medical records could lead to information overload for health care professionals. In addition, some worry that, while sometimes providing information that can be used to defend against malpractice suits, electronic medical records may occasionally provide ammunition for lawsuits (Putre, 2011). Therefore, when evaluating electronic medical records as an intervention, appropriate dimensions for evaluation might include effects on clinical decision making and legal implications.

Textbox 5.1 describes an example of a Base Case.

Textbox 5.1: Base Case Example

Sacramento-San Joaquin Delta flood control in California experiences several problems. Prior to intervening in the flood control system, a Base Case should be developed describing the current situation. The Base Case might include the following points (adapted from Lund et al., 2010). First, the delta is important because it is the largest single source of water in California for households and agriculture and because, as the largest estuary on the West Coast of the Americas, it is home to many important fish and animal species. Second, the delta (Where?) is in crisis because of sea-level rises, climate change, land use in the delta, and water exports to other parts of California. (These factors are the "hoW?" the problem came about and possible targets of interventions to address the problem, the "Whats?") The symptoms of crisis include fish species are crashing, water quality is worsening, and the risk of levee failure is increasing. (These outcomes are the "Whys?" and reflect what the interventions are supposed to accomplish.)

This Base Case suggests that alternative interventions to the delta crisis should be evaluated according to four dimensions:

- What will the interventions mean for water quality?
- What will the interventions mean for the ecosystem, particularly fish?
- How will the interventions affect land use in the delta, for example, use of the land for agriculture, recreation, and urban expansion, and the potential economic impacts of change?
- How will the interventions affect water exports out of the delta and the economic impacts of change?

(Adapted from Lund et al., 2010)

Activity 5.2 Generate Alternative Recommended Interventions

The next activity is to identify a set of alternatives to the Base (do nothing) Case that you will later evaluate. Again, for manageability, the number of interventions you identify here should probably be four or fewer.

Your best guide to identifying a set of alternatives is your theory of the problem, the "hoW?" of the Policy Problem Change Wheel. For the Sacramento-San Joaquin Delta problem described in Textbox 5.1, three "hoWs?" were offered: (1) sea-level rises and climate change, (2) land use, and (3) water exports. For each "hoW?," an intervention was recommended leading to three alternative recommended interventions: (1) stop exporting water from the delta, (2) build a peripheral canal for water exports, or (3) combine the current practice of pumping export water through the delta with a peripheral canal (Lund et al., 2010).

The set of alternative interventions should include one or two interventions that your evidence indicates will likely solve the policy problem. Lund and colleagues (2010) had evidence for all three interventions. As another example, if your policy problem is how to best increase water availability for crop irrigation in an African village, your synthesis of the evidence may reveal four alternatives to the Base Case: (1) reintroduce or reinforce indigenous water-management practices, (2) build a new "merry-go-round" well in the village, (3) maintain an existing village well that has become inoperable, and (4) increase farmers' access to privately owned treadle (foot) pumps. All four interventions should be in the set you analyze later.

Your selection of a set of alternatives should also take into account the malleability of the STORM context conditions related to your interventions. Remember that, in Chapter 1, we pointed out that some environmental conditions are easier to change than others. If you want your interventions to work, you need to recommend interventions that do not depend on changing conditions that are not malleable. For example, reintroducing indigenous water management practices may require men to do the work. If the men have left the villages to find work in the cities, and if the likelihood of getting them back to the villages is extremely low, then you may decide to drop that intervention altogether from the set you consider further. If the chances of the men returning are reasonable, but by no means certain, then you'd probably include this alternative in your evaluation but note the uncertainty in your evaluation of alternatives.

The set of alternative interventions should also include ones for which there is the strongest stakeholder support, even if the evidence suggests that those with strong stakeholder support are not particularly effective at solving the problem. (If the evidence suggests that a key stakeholder's preferred intervention is ineffective, you'll have a chance to point that out when you do Activity 5.3. For example, if your policy problem is how to prevent teen pregnancy, your alternatives to the Base Case might be (1) conduct sex education, (2) initiate a condom-distribution program, (3) combine sex education with a condom-distribution program, and (4) sponsor an abstinence program, with the fourth one included not because evidence indicated it was effective but because it is strongly advocated by social conservatives.

In the ideal case, your alternative recommended interventions will be what is sometimes called *MECE* (pronounced me-see), which stands for Mutually

Exclusive and Collectively Exhaustive. This means that the alternatives do not overlap so that differences between the alternatives are very clear (they are mutually exclusive), and the set of alternatives exhausts the range of possible alternatives. It will not always be possible to generate a MECE set of alternatives, but it is a goal to strive for.

Sometimes, it is a straightforward process to generate alternatives from your theory of the problem, from the evidence you synthesized or obtained, and from stakeholders' proposals, as in the examples above. But sometimes, especially when the evidence is very thin, you will need to generate alternative interventions creatively from scratch. Here, you may find it useful to consider three generic strategies that are often used for designing alternative interventions:

1. a *big-bang* or radical intervention

2. an *incremental* intervention—relatively small and possibly repeated changes in one aspect of the situation

3. *complementary* interventions—a set of coordinated changes in many aspects of the situation at once

Each one of these generic strategies has a different theory of "hoW?" it works and different pros and cons.

Big-Bang Interventions

The idea behind a big-bang intervention is that big problems demand big solutions. For example, suppose you aim to eliminate the practice of managers of multinational corporations paying bribes in exchange for permission to do business in a developing country. The United Kingdom (UK) recently implemented a big-bang intervention to combat this practice. It passed a tough new law making corporate officers responsible and subject to prosecution in the UK for corrupt dealings by any of their affiliate companies anywhere in the world. Other examples of big-bang interventions are nuclear power plants, large software projects, and new entitlement programs or major reforms in entitlement programs like Medicare and Social Security.

Big-bang interventions often look good because they appear likely to solve a problem once and for all. However, it is often very difficult to implement big-bang interventions. First, they are costly and often take a long time to develop. This means that there can be long delays before the benefits are achieved, allowing the costs of the current situation to accumulate. Second, they often affect so many stakeholder groups that there is almost always major opposition to them. Third, big-bang interventions often have negative side effects. For example, multinational companies might move their headquarters from the UK to another country to avoid complying with the new anticorruption law. Finally, big-bang solutions are often difficult, if not impossible, to reverse if they don't deliver the expected benefits or if the negative side effects are too great.

Incremental Interventions

An incremental intervention operates similarly to the principle of compound interest on money you've deposited in a bank account. You may only get a small amount of money (or improvement) in each time period; over time, however, these small improvements can add up to big results. Two examples of incremental solutions to the problem of petty corruption (pervasive demanding of, or offering, small gifts and bribes for doing what an official is supposed to do anyway) are shown in Textboxes 5.2 and 5.3. Experts believe that petty corruption greatly obstructs economic development. But attempting to eliminate petty corruption by criminalizing it (a big-bang solution) blames the victims and is unlikely to work because a major cause of petty corruption is jobs that don't pay a living wage. As shown in Textbox 5.2, one organization attempted to attack petty corruption in India by distributing zero rupee notes, which people could give to those who ask them to pay a bribe. This worthless money worked by shaming the recipient, which can often be more effective than any attempt at official punishment.

Textbox 5.2: Bribe Fighter: The Zero Rupee Note

"The zero rupee note is . . . a low-cost, low-tech solution that works from the bottom up. . . . The first batch of 25,000 was given away in 2007 [after] 90-minute teach-ins to educate people about the problem of corruption. . . . Soon, people began coming back with success stories, and asking for more zero rupee notes to use. . . .

"Raj Rajkumar, a small businessman . . . is among those who have used the zero rupee note successfully. . . . [When he and six other trustees arrived at a registry office to set up a nonprofit charity] the clerk told them that there were some 'formalities' that might hold up processing the application unless the group handed over 3,000 rupees (about $70) 'for tea.'

(Continued)

(Continued)

"Instead of handing the clerk the money, he slipped him the zero rupee note. The dumbstruck clerk, Rajkumar said, looked at the note and initially insisted that he was only asking for 'a tip,' not a bribe. But when the supervising registrar overheard the conversation and examined the zero rupee bill, she immediately ordered the clerk to process the charity's certification. 'Later the registrar told us that this was the very first trust that had ever been registered without having to pay a bribe,' Rajkumar said."

Kahn (2010)

The second example of an incremental intervention for dealing with petty corruption concerns the practice of offering small, unsolicited, nonmonetary gifts to civil servants or businesspeople who provide needed services, as shown in Textbox 5.3. Simply refusing these gifts may not be a good option because doing so can give offense: It may be contrary to local culture. But accepting such gifts is problematic too because, even if the gift is not intended as a bribe, the giver may still hope to get special treatment. One businessman in Africa managed to end the practice of being offered gifts by raffling off the gifts he received to his employees. When word got out, no more gifts were offered. But the businessman had avoided giving personal offense.

Textbox 5.3: Gift Killer: The Company Raffle

"Obviously a ballpoint or fountain pen—assuming it is not a chic designer model—is not in the same class as computer equipment given for private use or airfare to coveted destinations.

"In my experience a good way to stay clear of any suspicion of corruptibility is to have the gifts that employees have been given personally turned over to the company and made available to everyone—through a raffle, for example. During an assignment in a developing country in Africa I was, to my utter surprise, showered with gifts. At the end of my first year I had them put on display in the company conference room, numbered, and raffled off among the full workforce. In this way everyone from the night watchman to

> the secretaries to management staff got the chance to acquire desirable items that would otherwise have been beyond their means.
>
> "Most of the gifts came from customers who knew that a certain discretionary elbow room existed where the provision of goods in short supply (on account of lacking import licenses) or the granting of discounts were concerned. Without wishing to insinuate that our customers hoped to point me in a certain direction with their gifts, I can report that there were no more gifts once the word had got around how they had been disposed of."
>
> Leisinger (1998, p. 121)

Incremental solutions can often be inexpensive to implement and may require only local support. This means they often stay under the radar of stakeholder groups likely to oppose them. Later, if the incremental solutions produce good results, enthusiasm for change may grow and political opposition may be easily overcome. If incremental solutions don't work as expected, they are often easy to undo quietly, without damaging the reputations of the policy makers who supported them. On the other hand, incremental interventions may not work fast enough to prevent the harms of the current situation from accumulating unacceptably, and they may not be possible in some situations (e.g., flood control).

Complementary Interventions

The complementary interventions approach is based on the idea that, in order for change to stick, coordinated interventions need to be made simultaneously in several different aspects of the current situation, not just one. The example of corruption at the national or corporate level might make this strategy clearer. Some experts say that fighting corruption in countries involves "eight pillars" (Stapenhurst & Langseth, 1997):

1. Public-sector anticorruption strategies

2. Watchdog agencies

3. Public participation in the democratic process

4. Public awareness of the role of civil society

5. Accountability of the judicial system

6. The media

7. Private-sector and international business

8. International cooperation

Although some countries may be tempted to focus their corruption-fighting efforts on only one of these pillars, that approach is unlikely to succeed because the pillars are interdependent. If a country's legislature passes tough anticorruption legislation, this legislation is likely to have little effect unless there is an agency (or the media) that monitors compliance with the legislation and unless there is effective enforcement of the legislation in the courts. Furthermore, there are many ways that each of the pillars can be involved in anticorruption efforts. Examples include ethical codes, improved compensation for public-sector employees (reducing their incentives to take bribes), civil service reform, better training, financial management and audit procedures, disclosure of gifts, better procurement practices, political independence of watchdog agencies, and so forth. Would any one of these interventions alone be sufficient to reduce corruption significantly? That seems unlikely.

A similar situation exists in the case of corporate corruption. Think about what a company might have to do to comply effectively with the UK's tough anticorruption legislation. Corporate officers and directors have been urged to undertake comprehensive change programs that intervene in many areas of corporate practice simultaneously (Thomson Reuters Accelus, 2011). The list of actions, all of which companies may be urged to do, includes the following:

- Obtain board-level involvement in bribery compliance
- Undertake a periodic, documented risk assessment
- Undertake due diligence when hiring or contracting with people who perform services for the corporation
- Communicate policies widely within the organization, and implement training programs for employees
- Conduct monitoring activities and report regularly on the results
- Review and revamp policies regarding procurement, entertainment, and so forth

The complementary interventions approach is believed to work through reinforcement. One drawback is that it is difficult to achieve the cooperation of the many different stakeholders (e.g., the board of directors, purchasing officers, human resources management specialists, corporate communications specialists, auditors) needed to implement all facets of a complementary intervention program. Another drawback is the potential to create heavy-handed controls and inflexible procedures that ironically result in the very problems that you were trying to solve—a classic case of adverse effects!

Exerting too much control over people tends to promote fraud. Inflexible regulations make it more difficult for people to do business and encourage them to cut corners. "When reformist politicians enact laws to crack down on corporate crime, they set in train a process which in the final analysis may well serve the interest of the corporate criminals they seek to catch. This happens because the whole web of company law becomes more complex" (Braithwaite, 1979 pp. 129–130). As an example, New York City's contracting rules were put into place in order to avoid a repeat of a notorious corruption scandal. But the rules became so difficult to comply with that the city may have lost the hoped-for benefits of low costs and few ties to organized crime: "In part, contractor fraud is a consequence of policies that have produced a dysfunctional relationship between the city and contractors who know how to exploit a labyrinthine, suspicion-ridden, and inefficient contracting system" (Anechiarico & Jacobs, 1995).

To avoid inflexible interventions that end up perpetuating or reinforcing the problems they were meant to solve, two strategies are useful. One strategy is the use of interventions that attack more than one pillar or dimension of the problem simultaneously. For example, civil service reform can help prevent corruption by (1) formalizing codes of behavior, (2) improving selection of qualified candidates, AND (3) standardizing (and hopefully improving) pay scales for civil servants. A second strategy is the use of cultural interventions along with legalistic rules and punishments. *Cultural interventions* include leaders modeling appropriate behavior for employees, providing training and education in values and norms of behavior, publicly disclosing problems, and discussing how employees should respond when problems arise.

To summarize, if you have to design alternative interventions from scratch, the use of the three generic change strategies of big-bang, incremental, and complementary interventions can be a guide. Table 5.1 summarizes the pros and cons of each of the strategies. It's important to be aware of these pros and cons because, in the next activity of the Design Policy Recommendations Phase, you will have to evaluate the entire set of alternatives against criteria that include these pros and cons.

Activity 5.3 Evaluate the Set of Alternative Interventions

Once you have your alternative interventions, you should evaluate each one. It is important to do this fairly. Policy makers will see through any attempts to stack the deck for the intervention you favor if you only show the advantages and not the costs or risks. Lining up the alternatives side by side with the Base

Intervention Type	Description	Pros	Cons
Big-Bang Intervention	A single, big program designed to achieve a radical improvement in outcomes	When it works as expected, it creates a big improvement in the situation	Costly; uncertain; involves delays; difficult to implement; often generates great political resistance; often results in negative side effects; difficult or impossible to reverse later
Incremental Intervention	An attempt to achieve small but repeated and cumulative improvements in a single aspect of a situation	Small improvements mount up over time; often inexpensive to implement; often does not require broad political support; easy to ramp up or reverse depending on results	Can take a long time to have the desired effect; even the accumulated results may not be sufficient to solve the problem
Complementary Interventions	Simultaneous interventions in several dimensions of a situation	Changes in each dimension can be incremental, but the simultaneous changes in multiple dimensions reinforce each other, overcoming inertia	Requires coordination and commitment of many different leaders; can create an inflexible and counterproductive situation

Table 5.1   Pros and Cons of Three Generic Change Strategies for Generating Alternative Interventions

Case and assessing them all on the same criteria help to assure the policy makers that they have been given a range of choices, one of which has the possibility of solving the problem at reasonable cost with minimal risks.

The criteria you generated at the time you developed the Base Case are the starting point for your evaluation of your interventions. For example, consider the problem of water for crop irrigation in an African village. Let's say that, based on evidence, you generated four alternative interventions ranging from the use of indigenous water-management practices to digging new wells. As you developed your Base Case, you identified the major evaluation criteria for deciding which interventions to recommend. The intervention should (1) provide needed improvement in water availability, (2) have feasible initial investment requirements, (3) have few operating requirements, (4) have minimal mainte- nance requirements, and (5) have cultural and environmental compatibility. Now, you evaluate the four interventions using these criteria.

Your evaluation might lead to the following conclusions: Indigenous water- management practices fit the cultural and environmental context (a pro of the solution) but may not be efficient enough to supply the needed water and may no longer be maintainable if many villagers have moved to cities (cons; Reij, 1991). "Merry-go-round" wells are fairly expensive to install (con), but grant funding may be available (pro), and they are effective to a depth of 100 meters and can be powered by village children who think they are playing a game (pros; Mukherjee, 2008). These new wells may eventually go to waste, though, if there are no plans and resources for repairing them (con; Pearce, 2009). A program to maintain existing wells may be inexpensive if village woman can be trained to maintain them (pro; Hoque, Aziz, Hasan, & Patwary, 1991), but some village wells may be damaged beyond repair and may have insufficient capacity (cons). Foot treadle pumps are cheap (less than $35), can be produced locally (stimulating the economy), and can be deployed by individual farm- ers, substantially increasing their crop yields (pros; Postel, 2001). To spread the innovation, though, would require creative marketing techniques (such as open-air movie demonstrations; Postel, 2001) and a micro-finance scheme to enable farmers to buy them (cons); also, the pumps are effective only to a certain depth (cons).

The analysis of the water irrigation alternatives, clearly, is fairly complex. To present this information in a way that would facilitate decision making, we recommend that you build a table that lines up all the alternatives (including the Base Case) and shows how each alternative fares (pro or con) on each dimension. (See Table 5.2 for an example.) Where you are uncertain or have questions about an evaluation, it's best to say so. If you have included an alternative because of stakeholder support, but there is no evidence for (or actually evidence against) its effectiveness, be sure to point this out.

Evaluation Dimensions	Base Case (Do Nothing)	Reinforce Indigenous Water Management	Build a New "Merry-Go-Round" Well	Restore and Maintain Inoperable Village Well	Distribute Foot Pumps to Farmers
Improvement in water availability	Negative: current situation likely to worsen because of drought	Uncertain increase, depends on rainfall	Adequate increase, if groundwater depth is less than 100 meters (pro)	Uncertain increase, depends on possible contamination of existing well water	Adequate increase for farmers with pumps, if water depth is low (pro)
Initial investment requirements	None	Men are needed to build the earthworks; most men have left to work in cities (con)	High initial investment (con), but grant assistance is likely to be available (pro)	Uncertain—some reconstruction may be required	Low, pumps are inexpensive (pro), but they are privately owned and operated, and therefore, a micro-finance scheme will be required (con)
Operating requirements	None	Low, once built (pro)	Low, can be powered by children (pro)	Low, women draw water as needed (pro)	Low, can be operated by women, effort similar to farm work (pro)
Maintenance requirements	None	Moderate, occasional labor required, except in case of flood conditions (pro)	No evidence	Low, if women can be trained to do maintenance (pro)	Low (pro)
Cultural Compatibility	No change	Consistent with traditional gender roles (pro)	Is this exploitive of children? (uncertain)	Probably consistent with traditional roles (pro)	Private ownership of pumps may undermine cooperation in the community (con)

Table 5.2 Evaluation of Water Management Alternatives for an African Village (Hypothetical)

The evaluation criteria of the Base Case are the starting point for your evaluation of alternative interventions, but you may need to augment those criteria. For example, if you design alternatives from scratch using one or more of the generic strategies discussed earlier (big-bang, incremental, and complementary interventions), you should include their pros and cons in your evaluation. And particularly when one of your alternatives is a big-bang intervention, the responsible thing to do is to be as specific as you can about its potential negative side effects.

You might object to discussing negative side effects, arguing that it's not a good idea to talk down a good solution to the problem by pointing out consequences that are unlikely to occur; after all, reasonable safety precautions will be taken. However, failing to give adequate consideration to potential risks of well-intended solutions is simply not responsible behavior for a policy researcher. Evidence shows that people routinely underestimate the probability and severity of rare events (Kahneman, 2011), and you won't have to think hard to come up with a list of events against which policy makers should probably have taken better precautions: Hurricanes, nuclear accidents, financial crises, and terrorist attacks are high on the list.

You might also object to discussing negative side effects by arguing that it's impossible to be specific about outcomes different from (even opposite to) the problem resolution outcome you intend to bring about. But in many cases, negative outcomes are completely obvious in hindsight; therefore, with a little creative thought, you should be able to foresee them. For example, economists have theories (with unfamiliar terms like *adverse selection* and *moral hazard*) to refer to possible negative outcomes for policy situations (e.g., insurance) in which some people have better information than others. In the case of U.S. health care reform, for example, it was argued that an insurance mandate was necessary because healthy people would be likely to opt out of buying insurance, making it too costly for insurers to provide coverage for the people who want and need it. Some people debate this theory as well as the wisdom of insurance mandates, but that is not the point. The point is that health care policy makers can easily anticipate at least one negative side effect of some alternative interventions in health policy. Similarly, if you think about it creatively, you will be able to do this too in your own policy research.

For example, the public is often able to predict unintended negative side effects to many proposed policy changes: If we build more roads to reduce traffic congestion, more people will drive, and congestion will go up. If we give people welfare benefits or unemployment insurance, they won't look for jobs. If we reward people for performing better than their fellow employees, cooperation in the workplace will deteriorate. Again, we are not saying that these or similar statements are true. The point, though, is that it is not difficult to envision plausible, unintended negative side effects in advance of implementing an intervention.

If the unintended side effects of an intervention are potentially catastrophic, you need to include them explicitly in your evaluation of alternatives. And when you begin the next activity in this phase (Activity 5.4: Generate and Evaluate Implementation Alternatives), you will need to be explicit about how to address potentially catastrophic risks.

You should document your evaluation of the alternative interventions—employing your Base Case evaluation criteria, the pros and cons of the generic intervention types (if used), and your specific assessment of possibly rare but plausible negative side effects—in a table like Table 5.2. Presenting the information side by side allows policy makers to quickly review the options and their pros and cons, which will help them decide on next steps. The evaluation table will be the centerpiece of your Policy Decision Document (Deliverable 5.1, discussed in more detail next), which you will give to your advisers and policy makers. After reviewing your Policy Decision Document, advisers or policy makers may eliminate an alternative, add one, or ask you to do further analysis of the ones you included. If one of the interventions is particularly complex or especially likely to be selected, you may be asked to generate and evaluate alternative ways to implement that intervention, which is the task of Activity 5.4.

Activity 5.4 Generate and Evaluate Implementation Alternatives

Generating and evaluating alternative ways of implementing an intervention is similar to generating and evaluating alternative interventions. You want to keep them manageable in number and as MECE as possible. The big difference is in the kind of questions you ask yourself when generating implementation alternatives.

To help generate implementation alternatives, you can ask yourself questions like these:

- *What should the specific features of the intervention be?* For example, should the peripheral delta canal be large or small in capacity? Which pumping technology should be used? If the intervention involves setting up charging stations for electric cars, a key feature is likely to be the stations' payment model, such as pay at the point of service or a subscription plan. If the intervention is health care insurance, a key feature is likely to be a mandate requiring citizens to buy the insurance. During your synthesis of the evidence, you are likely to have identified variations of the intervention that might make a difference for their effectiveness in your context—this is the time and place to revisit these variations and bring them into your analysis.

- *What should the scope of the intervention be?* For example, should it cover all children under the age of 5 or all children under the age of 15? The bigger the scope of an intervention, the larger the potential outcomes. But the bigger the scope, the riskier the project, and the more likely it is to fail. Therefore, you may decide to propose implementation alternatives that differ in scope.

- *Who should lead the project?* For example, can the invention be started by an existing organization or agency, or does a new organization need to be created? New organizations take time to set up, but new projects can create conflicting priorities for existing agencies. Your proposed implementation alternatives, then, may involve different organizational options or management plans.

- *What should the timing and phasing of the intervention be?* Can you make incremental improvements in the Base Case (e.g., better pumping technology for water exports through the delta) and wait and see whether fish recover before making the investment in a peripheral canal? Can you build a peripheral canal, continue through-pumping, and wait and see whether fish recover before making a decision to discontinue through-pumping? By answering questions like these, you can generate implementation alternatives that differ in timing or phasing. Timing, or phasing, is a particularly useful strategy to use when developing implementation alternatives for big-bang interventions. When a proposed intervention has uncertain benefits or involves hard-to-assess risks, you can reduce the costs of failure or the potential for negative side effects by recommending a series of phases to the intervention, with the first phase involving a pilot project before full-scale implementation. For example, can you try out the intervention in one school or school district before expanding it to the entire state? Can you try a shorter, more-focused training program for one job category before spreading the program to everyone in the organization? Pilot projects are a valuable way to gather more evidence about an intervention's effectiveness and implementation issues before making a large and very visible commitment. Further, evidence generated by a pilot project showing that the intervention succeeds in your context is a very important way to increase stakeholder commitment and overcome resistance to change.

Interventions that take a long time to build and become operational (e.g., canals, large information systems) pose particular challenges for policy makers, regardless of their costs, benefits, or risks. Even if the policy maker manages to convince stakeholders initially of a big project's merits, the long delay before project completion gives opponents opportunities to mobilize and stop the project in its tracks. Therefore, policy researchers should always look for ways to reduce the size, delay, and risk of any big solution recommended, although we admit that it's not always possible to find them. (Can you get any flood control benefits from a half-built Three Gorges Dam?)

An example of how to reduce the size, delay, and risk of a big solution is the *results-driven incrementalism* approach. This approach was developed as an alternative to the traditional big-bang approach to implementing customizable software packages (Fichman & Moses, 1999). In the traditional big-bang software approach, the technical work of software customization is broken up into phases that relate to technical components of the software—for example, the database, the application modules, the management reports, and so on. This means that the whole project has to be completed before people can use the software and get its benefits. And a large traditional software project can take years to finish!

In the incremental approach, the technical work is divided up into short—two- or three-month—phases, each of which is designed to deliver some sort of business benefit, even if the rest of the project is never completed. For example, the first phase might be designed to identify customer orders that cannot be fulfilled when there are raw materials shortages. The second phase might be designed to identify all the raw materials that must be ordered for a complex, custom, and one-time customer order. The third phase might be designed to identify and suggest solutions to situations in which customer orders exceed manufacturing capacity, and so forth.

This results-driven incrementalism approach is easily extended from software projects to many types of policy interventions. By delivering demonstrable benefits quickly, the incremental approach can generate powerful political support for the continuation of an intervention so that it can go on to deliver its full potential. Conversely, if early phases of the implementation fail to produce the expected results, the project can be cancelled quickly and quietly without ever becoming a full-blown disaster—something that every policy maker wants to avoid.

DESIGN PHASE DELIVERABLE

The one deliverable (but a big one!) of the Design Policy Recommendations Phase is a decision document comparing alternative interventions (or alternative ways to implement a single intervention). This decision document lays the issues and alternatives out in a simple and logical fashion that helps policy makers decide to take action.

Deliverable 5.1 Policy Decision Document

After designing and evaluating intervention alternatives or the implementation alternatives of one intervention, you should draft a short, well-structured discussion document. This document presents your Base Case, your manageable set of intervention (or implementation) alternatives, and evaluations of each of the intervention (or implementation) alternatives. A good mental image of what is needed here is the kind of analysis that the League of Women Voters distributes prior to ballot initiatives. The league carefully (but briefly!) presents both the pros and the cons of each ballot initiative to facilitate decision making with the best available evidence.

The Policy Decision Document does not need to be long—and indeed it should not be long if you want policy makers to read it and to be influenced by your analysis. By all means, use tables and diagrams to make the document easy to read. If details are needed to support your points, include them in appendices. Table 5.3 offers an example outline of a Policy Decision Document.

CONCLUSIONS

The Design Policy Recommendations Phase is a big moment in the policy research process—the point at which policy makers begin to commit to a specific approach to solving a policy problem. The process is by no means

---

1. Introduction
    a. Brief description of the policy problem and why an intervention is needed
    b. Brief overview of the policy research approach
2. The Base Case
    a. Current situation
    b. Evidence of the problem (e.g., evidence that people are being harmed by the current situation)
    c. Criteria that should be used in evaluating alternative interventions
    d. Alternative interventions evaluated

(Continued)

(Continued)

3. Evaluation of alternative recommended interventions (or implementations)
   a. Alternative 1
      i. Description
      ii. Evaluation against the criteria (pros and cons)
   b. Alternative 2 (etc.)
4. Recommendations
   a. Comparing the alternatives to the Base Case (summarized in a table)
   b. Why no change is not (or is) an option
   c. Which of the alternatives (if any) deserves selection

Table 5.3   Sample Outline for Policy Decision Document (Alternative Interventions)

over at this point. Much work remains to expand stakeholder engagement and to generate widespread support for a particular course of action. (See Chapter 6.) In the course of this expanded engagement, the set of recommended alternative interventions may be altered, some may be dropped and new ones added, and the intervention preferred by policy makers may also change. In consequence, the decisions that result from the Design Policy Recommendations Phase are provisional and subject to change. But it is at this phase of the process that the policy researcher has the greatest opportunity to influence policy decision making. So make the most of it by designing a good set of alternative policy recommendations!

EXERCISES

1. Summarize the Base Case for your policy problem. What are the criteria against which alternative interventions should be evaluated?

2. Design three alternative interventions for your policy problem. Evaluate the alternatives against the evaluation criteria.

3. Take one of your three alternative interventions. Describe three different ways of implementing the intervention. What criteria should you use to evaluate the implementation alternatives? What are the pros and cons of each implementation alternative?

6

Expand Stakeholder Engagement

SUMMARY

This chapter describes what you should do after you have developed your recommendations for policy change. In this phase, you expand stakeholder engagement in the policy change process and, ideally, obtain stakeholders' commitment for policy change. Stakeholder expansion is accomplished through iteratively developing and sharing a Case for Change. By *Case for Change,* we mean a set of messages about your evidence and recommendations that becomes, with feedback, so compelling that stakeholders support policy change and take action.

As you expand stakeholder engagement around your Case for Change, you will undoubtedly surface new stakeholder concerns and objections that did not arise in earlier phases. Although this push back can be discouraging, it can also suggest ways to make your recommendations even better and more likely to succeed. Therefore, the Expand Stakeholder Engagement Phase is an iterative process of listening and refining your recommendations and your Case for Change.

Let's talk a minute about advocacy. While some policy researchers argue that advocacy of a particular policy intervention is part of policy research (e.g., Cummins, Byers, & Pedrick, 2011), the Expand Stakeholder Engagement Phase is not advocacy per se. Rather, it's about sharing what you have learned in your policy research with stakeholders for the purposes of improving the recommendations or proposed ways of implementing them and improving the persuasiveness of your Case for Change. In other words, the purpose of this phase is to make sure that your descriptions of the problem (the Base Case) and of alternative solutions (your recommendations) will resonate with stakeholders, motivating them to act. In this phase, you should take your Case for Change to stakeholders with an open mind toward their reactions rather than trying to sell them on (advocate for) your Case for Change. You will learn as much from those who disagree with your recommendations as from those who support you.

The four key activities and three deliverables of the Expand Stakeholder Engagement Phase are shown in Figure 6.1.

EXPAND STAKEHOLDER ENGAGEMENT PHASE
TRACKING INDICATORS

You arrived at this phase because you completed the Design Policy Recommendations Phase. Completing that phase is a huge accomplishment. However, having recommendations for policy change is not the same thing as having agreement from others about policy change. Much work must still be done to obtain a decision or a commitment to proceed with your recommendations.

The ultimate determination that you have successfully completed this Expand Stakeholder Engagement Phase is a decision on the part of policy makers and stakeholders to implement your recommended policy changes. This decision may take the form of passed legislation, approval by a corporation's board of directors, or even the tacit agreement of a community group to move forward with a change that takes people's time and energy to achieve. However, you cannot control decisions made by others. So you shouldn't try to gauge your progress by other people's actions. Instead, we suggest two other ways to track how you're doing: (1) the degree to which the Case for Change is understandable by key decision makers and other stakeholders and (2) the degree to which the Case for Change is credible to those stakeholders.

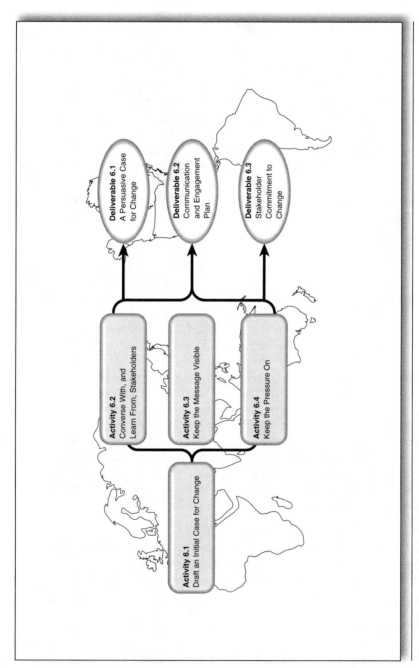

Figure 6.1 Expand Stakeholder Engagement Phase Voyage Map

Tracking Indicator 6.1 Understandability

Understandable Cases for Change are those that follow a logical sequence, make correct assumptions about what stakeholders know and don't know, use language and examples that the stakeholders are familiar with or can relate to, and draw conclusions that seem to flow naturally from the evidence. A Case for Change that is understandable does not have to be one that stakeholders agree to right from the start—that's an unrealistic expectation! Instead, you know that you are doing well when stakeholders can see and easily get your perspective on the problem. Reactions like "But why should I make this change," "I just don't get it," or "Aren't you assuming that . . ." indicate that you have not yet developed a good Case for Change and that you need to keep working on it to make it better.

Tracking Indicator 6.2 Credibility

Credible Cases for Change are based on evidence that is worthy of stakeholders' confidence. Stakeholders will have confidence in the evidence you present when they believe that you have not biased the evidence and when they can't explain away the evidence by challenging the rigor of your evidence synthesis or your research design for new evidence collection and analysis. For example, if you synthesized only evidence from highly biased sources related to a contentious right-to-life issue, stakeholders might question the credibility of your Case for Change. Or if your study examined only pregnant women from one religious faith, but you were trying to apply your findings to all women, then the credibility of your Case for Change might be questioned. Reactions from stakeholders like "Those findings are impossible," "Where could you have gotten that data," or "What you're telling me just doesn't feel right" indicate that your Case for Change is not yet credible.

Therefore, as you go through the activities involved in the Expand Stakeholder Engagement Phase, keep thinking about how you can improve the understandability and credibility of your Case for Change.

EXPAND STAKEHOLDER ENGAGEMENT
PHASE ACTIVITIES

Four activities will help you expand the engagement of your stakeholders:

Activity 6.1: Draft an Initial Case for Change

Activity 6.2: Converse With, and Learn From, Stakeholders

Activity 6.3: Keep the Message Visible

Activity 6.4: Keep the Pressure On

Activity 6.1 Draft an Initial Case for Change

In this activity, you draft your initial Case for Change. A Case for Change includes three presentation elements: (1) the policy problem you are investigating, including its prevalence and harmful outcomes; (2) evidence (both synthesized and newly obtained) about possible interventions to fix the problem; and (3) your policy recommendations. The key in presenting these three elements is to make them as simple, straightforward, logical, and credible as possible. Next, we give you suggestions for making this happen.

Use Numbers and Stories to Indicate Prevalence and Importance of Policy Problem. When you first explain the policy problem and its importance, use numbers that describe the prevalence of the problem and use anecdotes that illustrate the harms caused by the problem. If you are studying micro-finance programs for women in India, you might first tell a short, true story about a woman who was so poor before that she had made her 6-year-old son work so the family could eat, but how now, after getting a microloan, she has enough money to send her son to school. You could then follow up the story with numbers about how many poor women in India could realistically benefit from micro-financing. You may want the poor woman to tell the story herself, perhaps in a video. Short videos are excellent ways to present case examples because they are more convincing than stories told in your own words. Numbers about the prevalence of the problem should come from credible sources (e.g., the World Bank), which you would cite as data sources in your Case for Change.

Streamline Presentation of Most Essential Evidence. In presenting evidence, streamlining is critical because you will have compiled a lot of evidence, but your audience has a limited attention span. First, only present evidence that directly relates to your recommendations. Don't distract your stakeholders with interesting things you learned about the problem or solutions if these things are not now relevant to the Case for Change. (If you must include irrelevant evidence because stakeholders expect you to discuss it, mention it only in passing and explain why it isn't relevant.) Second, when you present evidence, present it in summary form such as "Out of 30 studies, 28 showed that malnutrition harms micro-financing success." (You can include a summary of all 30 studies in an appendix if that is necessary.) Third, describe anything that particularly stood out to you as surprising about the evidence or that you think would also be surprising to the audience. For example, if you were surprised by gender differences in micro-finance success rates, then you might summarize your findings in words like these: "Surprisingly, donors were more likely to make microloans to men than to women even though women are more likely than men to succeed in businesses financed by microloans." Fourth, be sure to tie (and to keep tying) your evidence to your recommendations; don't just present evidence relevant to your recommendations—tell stakeholders how the evidence supports your recommendations.

There are many different ways to present evidence about possible interventions. Usually, it's easier for the audience if you subdivide the evidence logically, for example, according to alternative theories of an intervention, phases of implementing an intervention, or context conditions affecting implementation success. For instance, providing micro-financing in developing countries involves (1) identifying and screening potential microloan recipients and (2) training the recipients selected for funding. These two phases might provide a logical way to subdivide your evidence about what makes micro-financing programs successful. Another logical way to subdivide the evidence about successful micro-financing programs might be (1) contextual conditions that help micro-finance programs succeed (e.g., government regulations, support by local banks) and (2) conditions that hinder micro-finance program success (e.g., malnutrition, local wars).

Table 6.1 summarizes our recommendations for presenting evidence.

Present Credible Policy Recommendations. Your Case for Change is built around the set of recommendations you developed in the Design Policy Recommendations Phase. These recommendations should be presented in as understandable and credible a fashion as possible in order to meet the criteria for this phase.

Recommendations are more credible when they make sense logically. How logically you can present your recommendations depends on how well you

---

- Use true stories to highlight the costs of the problem
- Use numbers to indicate the prevalence of the problem
- Discard evidence unrelated to your recommendation set
- Summarize evidence in as few words as possible
- Explicitly identify surprising evidence
- Tie evidence to recommendations
- Subdivide evidence logically

Table 6.1   Recommendations for Presenting Evidence in Your Case for Change

articulate your theory or causal model (the "hoW?" in the Policy Change Wheel) about the policy problem and the interventions. If the theory shows a causal effect on global warming that many would dispute, then the credibility of your recommendations may suffer—unless you've collected evidence to convince skeptics otherwise.

To present recommendations in a credible way, think through the different reasons a stakeholder might give to discredit your conclusions. Some of the reasons may be easy for you to overcome, especially if you have designed the policy research study or the synthesis carefully. For example, if you can envision a stakeholder claiming that the measures you used don't provide a good measurement of the important concepts, but you had thought through that issue in your design, you would be able to overcome that challenge. Provide your responses to these challenges in the Case for Change in a section that summarizes why you have confidence in the evidence. Don't phrase the section in a defensive manner ("You might think the measure isn't very good, but our design addressed all the issues you might have problems with"); use positive wording ("We took the following steps to increase our confidence in our evidence . . .").

If you can envision that some stakeholders will have trouble believing your evidence no matter how well you address their challenges, point out that your evidence is supported by others doing research in the field. Having your evidence corroborated by others is an excellent way to convince doubtful stakeholders.

Tie the evidence to the personal experiences of the people in your audience. For example, some policy research studies have found that sleep deprivation leads to diagnostic errors by medical students and interns. If you are trying to convince practicing physicians to consider reducing their own sleep deprivation, they may not be convinced by evidence about medical students and interns. Instead, try to find evidence specifically about sleep deprivation in doctors.

Credibility of recommendations is enhanced when the connections between the evidence and the recommendations are crystal clear. Graphical depictions are helpful in making that crystal-clear connection, such as the use of your causal model. For example, Richard Florida's (2005) policy study "The World Is Spiky," used spikes on a world map to depict population density: The higher the spikes, the greater the density. The viewer can see in a flash that the spikes are concentrated in urban areas. This image easily communicates the importance of fixing problems in urban areas.

Present Understandable Policy Recommendations. Following several suggestions will help you present your recommendations in an understandable manner. First, order the recommendations. You should explain the most general, comprehensive, and important recommendations first. Later,

present the additional recommendations needed for the more general recommendations to succeed.

Second, explain the recommendations in a logical fashion. For example, explaining your recommendations using the logic of the Policy Change Wheel will make them more understandable. If you were recommending a new agri-cultural technique for use by urban farmers, you would first explain what the intervention is ("What?") and what it is not ("What Not?"), the outcomes that will be achieved from the intervention ("Why?"), the explanation of how the intervention works ("hoW?"), the risks involved in doing the intervention ("Why Not?"), and the specific ways in which you plan to implement the intervention ("Who and Where?"). Let your audience be your guide for how much detail to provide about specific spokes in the Policy Change Wheel. Urban farmers being asked to adopt new agricultural techniques are likely to want more details about the "Why?," "What?," and "Who and Where?" of the intervention. For a legislator in the city, however, details of "What?" and "Who and Where?" may be less important than details about "Why?" and "Why Not?"

Consider creating a logo to make your message more understandable. If your message is that steps need to be taken to clean up urban blight (Florida, 2005), a logo of a world map with spikes at major cities is a nice visual image. The nonprofit organization Invisible Children uses a wonderful, simple image of a gun with children to symbolize the need to halt the use of child soldiers.

Be sure that your recommendations address the basic cognitive needs of your audience. Your audience wants to know exactly what your presentation means for them. To do this, follow the specific suggestions in Table 6.2 (collated from Koretz, 1982; Lipton, 1992; Smith & Robbins, 1982).

Summary: Making Recommendations Understandable and Credible. Put yourself in the shoes of your audience. In a technique called *mirroring,* excel-lent communicators learn the language, gestures, anecdotes, and examples that their listeners use regularly and then use those terms, gestures, and so on in presenting their own messages. Automobile sales associates are trained to quickly size you up in the showroom (Do you have kids? Do you use your auto for work? What is your current car?) and then tailor their message to you. If you have children, the sales associate might emphasize child safety locks and room for a child seat. If you have the same make of automobile from an earlier model year, the sales associate would emphasize the improvements in the newer version. If you "talk with your hands," the associate might too.

Research shows that people like people who are similar to them, so efforts to make yourself similar to the audience will help increase your credibility. But there are limits! If you really are different from your audience, too much mirror-ing will not seem genuine and will harm your credibility. In addition, you may

- Be concrete; use examples and anecdotes to make points personal and clear
- Be clear about what you want from your audience (support for the recommendation, feedback, understanding)
- Present your evidence-based recommendations first with evidence later
- Avoid using jargon
- Compare multiple options rather than presenting only one
- Clearly state your study's limitations
- Use section headings that convey your message; for example, don't use vague descriptive headlines (e.g., Parent Attendance Patterns), summarize your findings (e.g., Few Parents Attend PTA Meetings)
- Never use specialized language that might make your audience feel ignorant; conversely, never talk down to your audience ("I know you will find this difficult to understand" or "Let me put this simply . . .")
- Use a logo to concisely convey your message graphically

Table 6.2 Suggestions for Presenting Recommendations That Meet Audience Cognitive Needs

find it difficult to identify common experiences with your audience. If you have only lived in large urban areas and you are talking to farmers, you may find it useful to emphasize that you appreciate the value of hard labor and care of the land. But you should not push the similarities too far, or you will strain your credibility. And whatever you do, do not change your recommendations just to be telling your audience what you think they want to hear! What our suggestions are about is helping your audience hear what you are really trying to say.

Table 6.3 summarizes our suggestions for drafting your initial Case for Change.

Activity 6.2 Converse With, and Learn From, Stakeholders

When you communicate your evidence-based recommendations, you need to be in a learning, not a selling, mode. When you are trying to convince your audience to follow your recommendations, you are in a selling mode. What's wrong with that? After all, you have spent a lot more time thinking about this policy problem than they have, right? Wrong! Even though they may not have done systematic policy research, members of your audience have opinions about every spoke in your Policy Research Wheel. To find out what they are, you need to be in a learning mode.

- Order recommendations from most general, comprehensive, and important to most detailed
- Make connections between evidence and recommendations crystal clear
- Use graphs to present evidence for recommendations
- Include positively worded reasons why you believe your evidence is credible
- Tie evidence to the personal experiences of the audience
- Explain recommendations using the Policy Change Wheel
- Tie the level of detail about recommendations to the audience
- Ensure your presentation meets cognitive needs (state what you want, don't talk down, use examples)
- Mirror the audience when you can; otherwise, establish your similarities to the audience to the extent that you can

Table 6.3   Summary of Suggestions for Activity 6.3: Draft an Initial Case for Change

At this stage in the policy research process, you still have a lot to learn. You need to know about the roadblocks your recommended intervention might encounter if it were adopted. For example, you might need to learn that there are certain times of the year to avoid when implementing an agricultural intervention (e.g., because of a festival), that there are particular phrases or rationales that will alienate the farmers (e.g., "The government thinks this is good for you"), or that the farmers are lacking some resources needed for the intervention (e.g., plentiful water).

You also need to learn ways to help your recommended interventions succeed. Are there farmers who have successfully tried new practices in the past and therefore might be willing to try out your intervention? Did the farmers try something similar to your intervention before, and if so, what happened? Are there additional reasons for farmers to support your implementation? Is there a particular time of year, type of crop, or location that would be better to pilot test your ideas? For example, by engaging the audience, you may learn that each individual farmer decides when to plant, how to plant, what to plant, and how to care for the planted seeds. This information can tell you that you need to take into account variations in how the intervention will be implemented.

You also need to learn how your audience reacts to your presentation. Did they seem to understand what you were trying to convey? Did they act engaged? Did they realize the importance to them personally? Did they volunteer to help? Did they ask questions you thought you had already answered? Is there anything you could do to improve the understandability of the presentation? If your presentation did not engage the audience (e.g., they asked no questions, showed no interest), it is your responsibility to make it more engaging.

How could you do that? Instead of doing a classroom-type presentation with PowerPoint slides, you might make a model of the new agricultural practice. Instead of using bare statistics, you might use graphs and anecdotes to illustrate your evidence. Instead of you doing all the talking, invite members of the audience to describe the problems they've experienced with the old agricultural method. There are many ways to engage an audience.

If you fail to engage the audience, you are likely to encounter problems. You won't know how the audience really feels about the intervention. You may walk away with the mistaken impression that everyone agrees with you, when in fact they just kept their disagreements to themselves. Furthermore, you won't know why they disagree with your recommendations. People may disagree because they don't understand, because they misunderstand (understand wrongly), or because they understand quite well but think you are wrong. To improve your Case for Change, you need to learn why people disagree with you when they do. Finally, if you don't engage your audience, they may think you don't really care how they feel. By spending the extra time to figure out how to engage them, you demonstrate how much you value their opinions.

Over time, you will have to share your policy recommendations with several different audiences. Each one may need to hear your message in a different way. When the executives of well-run companies develop new strategies, they spend lots of time "on the road" talking to employees, customers, and suppliers about the new strategy and how to make it a reality. People in the company's corporate headquarters will have different opinions and concerns than people in manufacturing facilities in India or people in the research and development laboratory in Ireland. As the executive travels and talks with his or her key stakeholders, he or she will take notes of people's comments, questions, and concerns. He or she may modify (tweak) the presentation each time he or she gives it, making it stronger and stronger. You can do the same. After each presentation you give, think about what you learned and what changes you need to make the next time. Table 6.4 summarizes our suggestions for conversing with, and learning from, stakeholders.

Activity 6.3 Keep the Message Visible

Policy makers and other stakeholders are very busy people. Consequently, they may learn something from you one day and forget it the next. You need to keep your message visible. Marketing companies keep their messages

- Engage stakeholders when presenting your recommendations
- Learn from each presentation about possible intervention roadblocks and enablers
- Learn from each presentation how to improve the presentation and stakeholder engagement

Table 6.4 Suggestions for Conversing With, and Learning From, Stakeholders

visible to consumers through multiple *touch points:* repeated communications using different media, or *channels.* You can use a similar approach. One touch point may be a long, written document (a *white paper*) describing your evidence-based recommendations. Other touch points can include physical models or simulations of the intervention; one-page information sheets; e-mails, texts, blogs, or microblogs (e.g., using tools like Twitter); video clips like those posted on YouTube; websites—either within social networking platforms (e.g., Facebook) or with low-cost hosting services (e.g., Google); in-person presentations; virtual presentations (e.g., using tools like Webex); PowerPoint "slide decks" (presentation materials without real-time delivery available for people to download and review); small-group discussions (either in person or via the web). There are many touch points to choose from!

The general rule of thumb is to use as many touch points as possible. If you can, keep your presentations brief by putting detailed appendices on a website. If people seek out the appendices, you've had a second touch point! If your audience is Internet savvy, using social networking sites like Facebook will be enormously influential. If members of your target audience do not have access to the Internet or do not read, you will need visual touch points like physical models or videos. But developing these materials may also give you an extra touch point with people for who generally prefer to get their information in written reports.

You can use multiple touch points in ways that complement each other. You can use microblogging to "telegraph" new information related to your recommendations and to provide a link to a website for more information. You can use social networking tools to figure out how many supporters you have and who they are. Allowing people to post comments on your blog can give you feedback on how to better shape your message. If you are a creative person, consider interactive storytelling, in which you encourage people to complete a story about how your intervention would turn out.

The United Nations Children's Fund (UNICEF) uses many touch points to increase awareness of, and support for, its programs to improve the health, protection, and education of women and children worldwide. A great employer of social media, UNICEF carries channels on YouTube, Flickr, and Scribd and holds accounts in Facebook, MySpace, and Twitter. In addition, UNICEF maintains its own television, radio, podcast, and vodcast channels. UNICEF has touch points in a variety of languages including English, Spanish, French, and Arabic. A particularly moving touch point is the photo essay in which UNICEF employs photography to highlight sensitive topics such as pediatric HIV/AIDS in Zambia. UNICEF (2012) also puts research findings into easily understood documents with charts and graphs. See, for example, the executive summary of a much longer research report on "The State of the World's Children." All these touch points help members of the international community keep up with what's going on at UNICEF and establish an emotional connection to the organization.

Policy makers typically face many policy problems at the same time, so it's hard to get their attention. It's important to synchronize your touch points with their decision-making calendars—for example, a semiannual process for reviewing grant proposals and making awards. If you present your evidence-based recommendations at the wrong time, they may be ignored or forgotten when the time comes to make a decision. You should make a point of staying informed about the decision-making calendar. Check with policy makers' staff members to learn what they are concerned about now and whether advocacy groups are actively working an issue.

Table 6.5 summarizes our suggestions for keeping your message visible.

Activity 6.4 Keep the Pressure On

Policy making is an inherently chaotic activity. Constituents shift attention, dragging policy makers' attention with them. Policy makers are forced to

---

- Use multiple touch points including websites and social media tools to keep the issue and your recommendations in front of policy makers
- Keep your basic messages simple; use links to provide details
- Learn when critical decisions relevant to your policy problem are likely to be made

---

Table 6.5   Suggestions for Activity 6.3: Keep the Message Visible

make decisions with imperfect information. Policy makers must consider the positions of groups that fund their reelection campaigns, recognizing the severe personal cost of opposing these groups. Policies may become pawns in compromises on unrelated issues.

How can you use your policy research findings to catalyze decision making when you have no funding for their campaigns, when you don't represent a powerful constituent, and when your policy problem is not the one currently claiming the spotlight? The answer is this: Make use of the resources you do have. And one major resource you do have is your focused attention on your policy problem. While policy makers' attention shifts, you have been following the trends, you know the issues raised, you have observed the shifting alliances among stakeholders, and you are aware of the opportunities for interventions. Your steadfast focus on the policy problem can help keep policy makers on your course.

Another resource is your knowledge of the stakeholders (through your stakeholder analysis), which is reflected in the way you crafted your recommendations. By finding common ground, you show the policy maker how to achieve consensus.

Another resource is your evidence. The more deeply you understand your evidence, the better you are able to confidently judge whether the evidence will support changing the recommendations in ways that will boost consensus. The fact that you may be able to provide evidence to support two different alternatives makes your guidance invaluable to policy makers.

Depending on how you manage your touch points, you may have an additional resource: the collective wisdom of the crowd, obtained through your touch points. Simply creating touch points is not sufficient; they must be kept fresh and ready for the time when your evidence is needed. This means that you and your supporters must identify ways to keep your policy research and recommendations front and center for the policy makers. If you simply direct policy makers to a website or provide e-mails and one-page information sheets that contain information that they've already seen, you will be ignored.

One way to keep touch point fresh is to ask those afflicted by a policy problem to provide regular updates about their circumstances. The KatrinaWiki kept the plight of displaced New Orleans residents in the public eye by posting the names of people who were still looking for relatives weeks after the tragedy. Another way to keep the touch points fresh is to release additional conclusions (via e-mails, short memos, or microblogs) as you continue your analysis of policy research data. Keeping the dialogue open and active sends a much more powerful message to policy makers—that people care about this problem— than writing another report. You can keep a touch point fresh by aggregating and making links to research performed on your policy problem by reputable other policy researchers. Sites that aggregate policy research from multiple sources can be found for many problems. For example, the U.S. Environmental Protection Agency (EPA) functions as an aggregator on many policy problems, including avian flu and acid rain.

A final resource is your knowledge of the Policy Change Wheel, which helps you educate others about the nature of the policy problem and its potential solutions. Education is needed particularly when an audience does not see the policy problem in the same way that you do. The audience may not see that a problem exists at all. For example, although the United Nations' Intergovernmental Panel on Climate Change (IPCC) has concluded from a great deal of evidence that humans have played a role in global warming (IPCC, 2012), some scientists voiced their disagreements with both the evidence and the conclusions in a *Wall Street Journal* editorial ("No Need to Panic About Global Warming," 2012). In response, another scientist wrote an article that aimed to educate the public about "Why the Global Warming Skeptics Are Wrong" (Nordhaus, 2012).

Even if the audience accepts that a problem exists, they may not appreciate the severity of a policy problem like potential flooding in the Maldive Islands. Or the audience may not believe that the policy problem will result in the harms you project, as in the case of melting Arctic sea ice. Finally, the audience may argue that the costs of fixing a policy problem outweigh the costs of the problem—an argument offered for the U.S. failure to sign the International Global Warming Treaty.

When you have an audience that is not engaged because they do not see the problem in the same way that you do, education is required. However, successful education can only come from people believed—by the unengaged stakeholders—to be credible educators. Because you already see that there is a problem, you are by definition not a credible educator for such an audience. Instead, you must enlist the help of those who are credible to the audience (e.g., religious leaders, local community leaders, leaders of their political party, previously outspoken critics). You need to identify potential credible educators who are close to changing their minds. Such a person might have both a personal connection (e.g., a kinship relation, a shared hobby or sport) to those who need to be educated and a relevant, recent personal experience (e.g., a trip to the Maldives or the Arctic). Finding credible educators and then providing them with your evidence can be a powerful resource for policy change.

In sum, keeping the pressure on policy makers means not letting opposition to your recommendations slow you down. Keeping the pressure on means using all your resources to encourage change, even when policy makers resist it. Table 6.6 summarizes the resources you have to keep the pressure on policy makers.

- Use your interest and passion in the policy problem to follow trends, issues, and shifting alliances among stakeholders
- Offer policy makers the possibility of consensus building through your stakeholder analysis
- Offer modifications of your recommended policy options when they are supported by your evidence
- Keep the problem and possible interventions in front of policy makers by releasing your conclusions in waves
- Keep dialogue going about the policy problem
- Educate stakeholders on the comprehensive nature of the policy problem and possible interventions
- Enlist the help of those who have credible information about the policy problem and possible interventions

Table 6.6   Resources Available to You to Keep Pressure on Policy Makers

DELIVERABLES

Three deliverables complete this phase of the policy research process: (1) a persuasive Case for Change, (2) a communication and engagement plan, and (3) stakeholder commitment to change.

Deliverable 6.1 A Persuasive Case for Change

The Case for Change is a deliverable that can take a number of different forms. In business contexts, PowerPoint presentations are popular. In U.S. congressional hearings, written textual testimony is popular. Many stakeholders expect a lengthy, written report with a two- to three-page executive summary containing the recommendations. Table 6.7 shows an example outline for a persuasive Case for Change.

Deliverable 6.2 Communication and Engagement Plan

This chapter described a number of activities for engaging stakeholders. In Deliverable 6.2, you create a plan for performing some set of those activities. As the plan involves communicating with stakeholders, it is called a Communication Plan. Because the plan involves not simply communication

I. Title Page
- Title conveying the policy problem and general recommendations for intervention
- Authors and advisory group
- Logo

II. One- to Two-Page Executive Summary
- Summary of policy recommendations and rationale

III. Title Page (again)

IV. Policy Problem
- The Base Case (evidence of problem's importance)

V. Recommendations
- Most general recommendation plus evidence to support this recommendation
- Next most general recommendation plus evidence
- Other recommendations

VI. Appendix of Relevant Evidence

VII. Appendix of Policy Research Methodology

Table 6.7   Outline of Report Presenting a Persuasive Case for Change

but also engagement, we also call it an Engagement Plan. This deliverable is typically a one- to two-page memo and consists of the following elements:

- Goal of the Plan. Clarify what you want to accomplish from your Expand Stakeholder Engagement Phase activities. Do you want to change the stakeholders' attitudes, change their behaviors, or just get their advice?

- Key Targeted Stakeholders. Who are you targeting through these activities? These stakeholders are the audience. Your audience is likely to include several different stakeholder groups, each of which may need a separate plan.

- Profile of the Stakeholder Groups in Your Audience. Briefly describe the key values of each stakeholder group, where they get their information, and what type of information is more likely to be credible to them.

- Key Message-by-Stakeholder Group Matrix. For each stakeholder group, jot down the key messages you will provide. For legislators, your message might focus on cost reductions; for recipients of services, your message might focus on improved quality of life.

- Key Communication Channel-by-Stakeholder Group Matrix. The communication channels available to you may include presentations at supermarkets, malls, and community centers; handouts at employee meetings; executive briefings or informal meetings with decision makers; or radio talk shows, e-mail distribution LISTSERVs, dedicated websites, newspapers, blogs, and Twitter. Different stakeholders seek information in different ways; match your channels of communication to their preferences.

- Possible Partners. Identify who you might be able to enlist to help you in this engagement process, such as interested consultants, nonprofit organizations, or volunteer interns.

- Timeline. Decide which stakeholder group to approach first by which channel. Then, take the rest of the stakeholder groups in order.

Once you have your plan, you need to execute it. After every engagement, reflect on how it went, and correct your course if you need to.

Deliverable 6.3 Stakeholder Commitment to Change

It is unrealistic to expect that your policy research will always get policy makers to make the decisions and take the actions you recommend. But you can make an important difference with your policy research even in lesser ways. For example, your research may convince policy makers to publicly advocate the need for change (without necessarily committing to a particular kind of change). Even better is to convince policy makers to listen to the evidence about how various interventions have worked in other places. Better still is a commitment to devote resources to the policy area, such as for obtaining new evidence or conducting a pilot test of an intervention. Even when policy makers are not fully committed to the course of action you recommend, you still may be successful in increasing their commitment to policy change.

The activities described in this chapter are intended to help you increase policy makers' and other stakeholders' commitments to change. By drafting an understandable, credible, and persuasive Case for Change, you can increase stakeholders' understanding and belief, thus increasing their commitment. By learning from stakeholders as you present your recommendations, you mold your recommendations closer to their needs, thus increasing their commitment. By keeping the message visible, you are ready to pounce when the time for change is ripe. By keeping the pressure on, you engage stakeholders in the process of making a difference.

CONCLUSIONS

If you want to bring about a change of policy, you have to work hard to make your evidence known through multiple touch points, learn from your audiences, and mold your recommendations to their needs. You do this by taking your Case for Change "on the road." You may do this literally, by traveling around, meeting with and talking to your stakeholders wherever they are. You may do this figuratively, by aggregating the research and experiences of others. You may do this virtually, by means of websites, YouTube videos, and blogs about the policy problem and your evidence. Whether literal, figurative, or virtual, taking your Case for Change on the road should educate you as you educate others. It should help you fill gaps in your knowledge about the spokes of the Policy Change Wheel and about intervention roadblocks and enablers. It should give you new ideas for the next policy research project. It should bring you into contact with new partners and advisers. Finally, it should give you optimism and hope that there are others out there who care.

EXERCISES

1. Take a policy problem of interest to you, for example, health care reform, immigration, and so on. Find a recent statement made by a partisan of some intervention for solving the policy problem. Is the Case for Change in this statement understandable and credible? Justify your answer.

2. List three of the strongest objections to the proposed policy change. Present a counterargument to each of these objectives. Can you think of a way that the recommendation could be modified to accommodate those objections while still achieving its goals?

3. Draft a (more) persuasive Case for Change than the one in the partisan's statement.

4. Prepare a Communication and Engagement Plan: What stakeholder groups would you need to engage, and how would you engage each one?

7

Reflect on the Policy Research Voyage

SUMMARY

Policy research is about helping people take socially responsible action to improve our world by bringing together *evidence,* that is, facts established through careful procedures and analysis, and *meaning,* that is, values, opinions, and beliefs about what is important. Policy research is not an exact science and cannot be reduced to a set of systematic procedures. It is as much an art as it is a science, and doing it well takes practice-honed skill. To develop our skills, we must look back on what we did, reflect on what worked and what didn't work, and apply our learning to future projects.

As you gain experience in a particular policy research area, you will learn more about problems, their consequences, their possible solutions, and how and why problems come about and solutions work. But, even more important, through reflection on your experience, you will learn about the process of doing successful policy research. This learning will not only improve your understanding of one policy area and context. It will also help you apply your skills to other problems and contexts.

This chapter is intended to help you learn how to learn about the process of doing policy research. We distill the procedures we described in the previous six chapters into a set of principles for doing policy research. We invite you to think of these principles as a starting point, not as a hard and fast checklist. Revise them and add to them as you gain experience with policy research. And be sure to share your learning with others. Only by working together can we really make a difference with policy research.

Principles are prescriptive statements—recommendations—based on theories of cause–effect relationships about the means to produce some desired state of affairs. Based on our experience and our evidence-based theories about what makes for successful policy research, we offer you this starting set of principles to guide your learning about the policy research process.

Principle 1: Be creative.

Principle 2: Be responsible.

Principle 3: Iterate. (If at first you don't succeed, try, try again!)

Principle 4: Don't advocate; educate. (And be educated.)

Principle 5: Know when to hold; know when to fold.

Principle 6: Build your capacity to learn.

Principle 7: Pass on your policy knowledge to others.

Let's briefly consider each of these principles.

Principle 1 Be Creative

You won't get far in your attempts to change the world by following formulas. Throughout the previous six chapters, we discussed many ways in which creativity is required for effective policy research. They include the following:

- *Creativity in defining (and refining) policy research questions.* Creativity is needed because the questions that others pose for you may not be broad enough to allow you to envision new solutions. At the same time, you need creativity to keep the scope of investigation narrow enough to allow you to arrive at answers while satisfying stakeholders that you've addressed the issues of most importance to them. Creativity is needed because there is never enough time or money to work through the many different perspectives on important policy questions.

- *Creativity in analyzing policy research problems and potential interventions.* Creativity is needed because it's so easy to focus on the harms of the current situation and to ignore the possible harms that an intervention may cause. Creativity is needed because, as you learn more about a problem, your causal models of why the problem occurs and how to solve it can change. Creativity is needed because a solution that works elsewhere may not work in the particular STORM conditions of your context.

- *Creativity in synthesizing existing evidence.* Creativity is needed because the evidence may be patchy and weak. You may need to assemble a synthesis from fragments of evidence. Creativity is also needed to know how much confidence to have in the evidence or the synthesis you construct from it.

- *Creativity in designing new evidence collection.* Creativity is needed because you may not be able to find answers to your questions by conducting secondary analyses of data already stored in archives. You may need to interview or survey people, conduct a case study, or even perform a quasi-experiment. And creativity is needed to design such studies in ways that will yield useful answers while minimizing obvious flaws that could cause others to challenge your new evidence.

- *Creativity in designing alternative interventions or implementation alternatives.* Creativity in designing interventions may be needed for any number of reasons. There may be no hard evidence about the effectiveness and side effects of some solutions (e.g., deep-ocean carbon sequestration). Nothing may be known about how a generally effective intervention will work in your context. Something about your context is different enough that a new approach is needed for treatment delivery. How and why a solution works may be ambiguous until you try it. When it comes to interventions, the devil is in the details, and so is the likelihood of change for the better.

- *Creativity in developing persuasive cases for change.* Good ideas are never enough to change the world. People need motivations and reasons to make change. Finding (valid!) arguments that will resonate with different audiences is not easy to do, and there is no formula to follow.

From your own reading of the previous six chapters, you may have identified additional ways in which the policy research process requires creativity. Can you name one or two?

Principle 2 Be Responsible

An equally important principle is to be responsible. Again, we can identify a number of ways in which responsibility is essential to successful policy research. Perhaps you can identify more ways?

- *Responsibility in policy problem definition.* Responsibility may be needed because the way others defined a policy problem for you excludes STORM conditions or intervention possibilities that are critical for successful change. Clearly, you cannot afford to ignore the way others define the problem or the solution set. If you do, you may not survive to fight the next policy battle. At the same time, your primary commitment should be to solving policy problems, which cannot be done by ignoring the evidence. (To manage your relationships with stakeholders responsibly takes creativity too!)

- *Responsibility in your use of existing evidence.* You may win a battle but lose the war if you use only evidence that favors your point of view or if you fail to disclose evidence about the risks of an intervention you favor.

- *Responsibility in your collection of new evidence.* You need to protect human subjects from the risk of harm—such as physical or mental distress or loss of privacy—that may arise from your research procedures. Do not share any information that you learned in confidence because improperly sharing knowledge can ruin your ability to get information from other sources in the future.

- *Responsibility in your evaluation of alternative interventions or implementation alternatives.* Responsibility here means assessing all alternatives with the same criteria and considering the risks of interventions ("Why Not?") along with their benefits.

- *Responsibility in your communication and engagement with stakeholders.* When you customize your Case for Change for particular stakeholder groups, do you tell them what you think they want to hear, or do you tell them what they really need to know? For example, do you tell them that a voucher system may not fully compensate people for benefits they have today?

Here's an exercise for you: Name at least two other ways in which effective policy research involves responsibility.

Principle 3 Iterate (If at First You Don't Succeed, Try, Try Again!)

You might think that Principle 3 is just an extension of Principle 1: Be Creative. But iterating is often more a matter of hard work and stubbornness than of sheer flashes of insight. Iteration is needed for effectiveness in several parts of the policy research process.

- *Iteration in defining the policy research question.* If someone gives you a policy research question, it is very likely not to be the question that you most need to answer if you are going to make a difference with your policy research. Throughout this book, we have emphasized how important it is to revise your question as you learn more about the problem, about the STORM context conditions, and about the interventions and their costs, benefits, and risks.

- *Iteration in finding and synthesizing existing evidence.* When you familiarize yourself with a policy area, you will come across evidence that you do not then explore in depth. Later, you will return to these sources as you deepen your knowledge of the policy problem and interventions. This learning process needs to be continuous because you may come across existing evidence at any point in the policy research process.

- *Iteration in obtaining new evidence, particularly from quasi-experiments and pilot implementations.* OK, now you know how the intervention as practiced in Tokyo works in rural Alabama. Do you know everything you need to know to know to roll out a full-scale implementation of your intervention throughout the southern U.S. states? Probably not. To avoid the risks of failure or unintended consequences, you may need to iterate new evidence collection more than once.

In what other areas do you think the principle of iteration applies in effective policy research?

Principle 4 Don't Advocate; Educate (And Be Educated)

We readily acknowledge that there is a role for advocacy in changing the world. Many people chose this path. And it may sometimes be very effective in creating change. But policy research can make a difference, and advocacy is not the path of the policy researcher.

Policy research is the bridge between evidence (i.e., systematically derived facts) and meaning (i.e., values, opinions, beliefs, which includes pure advocacy of particular points of view). Policy researchers need to develop and maintain their reputation for straight talk. They need to stick to the facts and assess fairly how the facts square with stakeholders' meanings. A voucher program (as proposed by stakeholder Group X) may lower total government spending on entitlement programs. But it may also render a certain type of benefit (education, health care, etc.) out of reach for a certain population of vulnerable citizens (minorities, the elderly). As a policy researcher, versus an advocate, you have the responsibility to report on these trade-offs fair and square.

Advocates do not have the same responsibility. Anything goes for advocates. But policy researchers need to play fair, or they will lose their credibility. Policy research is the voice of reason in a polarized society. Policy researchers have a responsibility to educate the world about what they know based on their knowledge of the evidence and what the evidence means to various stakeholders.

The inverse of this principle is that policy researchers also have the responsibility to be educated by stakeholders. There is no room for closed minds among good policy researchers. You must always be willing to admit that you were wrong and that you now have a revised recommendation based on newly available evidence. Yes, following this principle may be a career-limiting move if you work for an advocacy organization. But if you work for a pure advocacy organization, you need to question your role. If you want to make a difference through policy research, we believe, you need an open mind.

Engaging directly with all relevant stakeholders is the best way we know to have, and to keep, an open mind. We know this is not an easy path. The policy makers we work with and for may have strong opinions and considerable means to influence us. The vulnerable stakeholders we hope to better may not applaud all of our findings or recommendations. But through the process of trying to educate others and allowing ourselves to be educated by others, we have the possibility of assembling new coalitions of stakeholders and arriving at new interventions that have resisted prior attempts to solve critical social problems. This is where effective policy research can help make the world a better place.

Principle 5 Know When to Hold; Know When to Fold

The somewhat facetious wording of this principle winks at a well-known American folk song about gambling. The basic idea is that gamblers need to know when to stay in a game (hold their cards) and when to walk away from it (fold their cards). We don't gamble, but we believe the basic principle applies to policy researchers. We need to know when to stand up for our principles and when to change our positions in ways that lead to change for the better.

Policy researchers have, and have to take, positions on issues. For instance, you may be confident about your knowledge of the causes of unemployment in the United States. Let's say you believe (based on your evidence and analysis) that the best solution to the problem is for American corporations to cease offshore outsourcing. This is not likely to be a popular recommendation! More pragmatic, but still consistent with your theory of the problem's causes and solutions, would be to recommend tax incentives for companies that hire American workers.

We believe that policy researchers should be pragmatic and willing to settle for less when doing so helps bring about change for the better. You can be pragmatic and willing to settle for less both in the scope of your research and in the recommendations you make. On the scope side, for example, you may not have the time and resources to answer the question of why urban youths turn to drug dealing. You may, however, be able to learn about interventions that turn urban youths away from drug dealing and toward legal ways of earning a living. This would be a huge contribution to policy knowledge, and you should be happy with your achievement, even if it is limited. Similarly, you may have learned that the best way to ensure that urban youths do not turn to drug dealing in the first place is to provide them with a certain level of guaranteed income. But you may understand that a more acceptable intervention politically is to provide urban youths with recreational facilities and job training programs. It is no sin to settle for less than what you believe to be best if that less makes a step in the right direction. Recommending an intermediate solution may help decision makers and the public embrace more change in the future as evidence about the effectiveness of the intervention accumulates.

Settling for less, in this sense, does not mean caving in to stakeholders. Rather, it means understanding that small wins sometimes add up to big gains. If you hold out for a grand solution, some stakeholders may be able block all change. Sometimes, the most responsible course of action is to recommend an intervention that is smaller than needed to really fix the problem but more likely to be accepted and have some positive effect.

Principle 6 Build Your Capacity to Learn

Policy research involves several learning loops. The first learning loop comes from the immediate feedback you receive as you consult your sources: documents, experts, and other stakeholders. With each source, you learn more about the policy problem and possible solutions. You jot down notes on the Policy Problem Change Wheel, scratch out those notes as you find new sources of evidence, and then add in more information that helps to synthesize the previous knowledge you had gained. As you implement a rigorous design for obtaining new evidence (as in Chapter 4), you learn and make adjustments based on how participants react to your questions or experiments.

This immediate feedback loop should continue throughout the policy research process. With each phase of the policy research voyage, the focus of learning shifts, so don't make the mistake of thinking that later phases involve less learning than earlier stages. In the Launch Phase, your focus is on familiarizing yourself about the policy problem, possible solutions, and sources of evidence. In the Synthesize Existing Evidence Phase, your focus is on learning about what is known and not known about problems and their solutions. In the Obtain New Evidence Phase, your focus is on learning more about research participants and their reactions to your questions or pilot interventions. In the Design Policy Recommendations Phase, your focus is learning about making recommendations that will be acceptable in your context and will actually solve policy problems. In the Expand Stakeholder Engagement Phase, your focus is on learning about messages that resonate with stakeholders. This type of learning is immediate and continuous.

The second learning cycle occurs at the end of each policy research phase and comes from reflecting on the feedback you receive on your research deliverables. The documents you produce in each phase of policy research are generally reviewed by three parties: your client, your targeted policy maker, and your formal or informal board of advisers. Your client is the person or organization that asked you to do policy research effort. Sometimes, your client and the targeted policy maker are the same person or organization. For example, the U.S. National Academy of Sciences often conducts policy research for the U.S. Congress; in this case, the client and policy maker are the same. Often, clients and policy makers are not the same. For example, a government agency may hire a consulting firm to provide policy advice. In this case, the government agency is the policy maker, and the consulting firm is your client. Your advisers are the third group to review your deliverables at the end of each phase. Because they are neither your client nor policy makers, they have very different perspectives. They may be more honest in their criticism of your deliverables and may offer more concrete advice about improving them.

After each phase, we suggest you conduct an After-Action Review, a common technique used by learning organizations. After-Action Reviews are designed to answer four questions:

1. What did you expect to happen?

2. What actually occurred?

3. What went well, and why?

4. What can be improved, and how?

You should ask these questions about both the substance of your deliverables and the process of producing them. Suppose, for example, you had expected to complete the Launch Phase in three days, and it took you three weeks. You had expected to get excellent feedback from your client on your deliverable, but instead, the client simply acknowledged its receipt. Clearly, there are differences here between what you expected and what occurred. Differences like these warrant your thinking about why they occurred and what you should do differently next time.

Perhaps the Launch Phase took so long because you didn't get good guidance from your client or you went too deep into the existing evidence. (On the other hand, maybe you were just unrealistic in your expectations about how long the Launch Phase would take!) You might conclude from this After-Action Review that you need to work more closely with your client in the next phase of the research or do a better job of finding experts to brief you the next time you launch a policy study.

The final and largest learning loop occurs at the end of a policy research project. Commonly referred to as a Lessons-Learned Review, this end-of-project reflection offers a unique opportunity for learning. Ideally, Lessons-Learned Reviews are conducted as meetings attended by all the policy researchers who worked on a project, the client, policy makers, and advisers. The questions posed in Lessons-Learned Reviews are generally similar to those of the After-Action Review, but they tend to be much more specific. Often, lessons are learned about technical matters such as the policy problem and interventions and about the process of doing policy research.

You can focus Lessons-Learned Reviews on the guidelines we provided for each policy research phase and the cross-cutting principles like *be creative* and *be responsible*. What actions did you find most useful for keeping stakeholders engaged over time? How did you know when creative new solutions were needed? How did you come to know that a particular intervention would be acceptable to a stakeholder? How did you skim all the literature in just a few days? Where did you find an expert on tuberculosis in China? Documenting your lessons learned and organizing them by the phase of the policy research process will ensure that you keep developing your skills for years to come.

Sometimes, what you learn from your policy research effort is not what you thought you were going to learn. For example, in the summer of 2010, Rebecca Niemiec, a Dartmouth College student passionate about sustainability, engaged in a policy research effort with 10 other Dartmouth students in which they researched sustainability solutions, gathered evidence supporting sustainability, developed educational material to promote sustainability, identified key policy

makers for and against sustainability, and then outfitted a coach bus to demonstrate sustainable transportation practices, including solar panels, bamboo
flooring, recycled countertops, and the use of purified vegetable oil as fuel. They
spent 10 weeks traveling across the United States sharing their knowledge of
sustainability. At the close of the 2010 tour aboard the Big Green Bus, Rebecca
realized that she had learned something quite unexpected from her tour. She had
expected that she would be reporting on how many people she had influenced
during the 10 weeks. Instead, she reflected on how much she had been influenced by the many she had encountered.

> I cannot count the amount of times that people have asked me, both on the road
> and since I've been back at Dartmouth, "So, do you think you've made a differ-
> ence?" After 11,000 miles, 34 states, 11 weeks, countless hours of preparation,
> and 14,869 website views I do know that. . . . One of the beautiful things about
> the bus is that it gives a voice to those around the country. So many people are
> working towards a sustainable future, but many think they are alone in their
> efforts. We are there to tell those stories. We listened and internalized and shared
> the stories of the people we met, from retired artists in New York reusing old art
> supplies to beautify their city, to a man in the backwoods of Maine who has spent
> the past 30 years designing a boat to sail around the world made solely of recycled
> materials. We met inner city kids who had convinced their families to use
> reusable water bottles, a high school student working alone to try and create a
> recycling program in her town, a family from Idaho producing their own biofuels
> in their backyard, a young couple designing their new house to be "off the grid,"
> a recent grad working to connect a local brewery restaurant and a local urban
> farm, and a lobbyist fighting day after day against the long slow processes of
> American politics to try to pass new energy legislation. All of their stories became
> our story as we traveled around the country, blogging and taking videos and
> sharing what we learned with media and all who would listen. All of these stories
> need to be told, because they represent our future. The stories became a part of
> me throughout the summer, and I know I understand America and myself a bit
> better because of them. I want to thank everyone who added a bit of their story to
> ours, because it is you who are making the difference. . . . We are only a vehicle
> for change. (Niemiec, 2010)

Principle 7 Pass on Your Policy Knowledge to Others

Some policy researchers focus exclusively on one policy problem for
years. More frequently, however, policy research is episodic. The clients of
professional policy researchers may have limited funding for research; policy
makers may have limited attention for a particular policy issue. Therefore,
professional policy researchers sometimes move on to other topics. Accidental

policy researchers often go back to their day jobs once they have completed their policy studies.

When policy researchers move on to other projects, they have a responsibility to pass on what they know to others—*downstreamers*—people who will continue to be involved in the policy problem in the future. Downstreamers may be policy makers such as politicians and funding agencies that are motivated to make decisions and take action based on policy research. Downstreamers may be social or business entrepreneurs who actually implement interventions. Downstreamers may be advocates who publicize policy problems and lobby for particular solutions.

When you pass on your knowledge to downstreamers, you should aim to convey not just the explicit knowledge recorded in your documents and deliverables but also your *tacit knowledge*—knowledge that is hard to write down. After a policy research project, you have a wealth of tacit knowledge, such as judgments about advisers who will be most helpful to downstreamers or hunches about new interventions about which no evidence exists. You should try to pass along these judgments and hunches, not just the recommendations and evidence you documented at the end. Why would a downstreamer find your tacit knowledge useful? Remember that, no matter how solid your research, your recommendations may still not work in practice. This means that the downstreamer will have to try something different to achieve the policy's intended objectives. Both your careful documentation in deliverables and the tacit knowledge you share informally will help downstreamers decide what to try next.

In addition to sharing your tacit knowledge, you should volunteer to serve as a sounding board for downstreamers and periodically meet with them to learn about what's happening. That way, you will accumulate new evidence about what works and what doesn't and deepen your knowledge of the policy domain. That knowledge will come in handy if you go back to policy research at some time in the future.

CONCLUSIONS

Reflection is a time for learning. You should be proud of what you have accomplished through your policy research but willing to admit that you still have lots to learn. You should always hold yourself to a high standard for learning. Say to yourself: Each time I do policy research, I will do it better and more responsibility. I will engage stakeholders better. I will get better at balancing meaningfulness and manageability. I will get better at spotting malleable variables in the STORM context and at spotting possible risks and harmful consequences of interventions. I will get better at designing recommendations that succeed both at gaining political acceptance and at really solving policy problems. I will get better at learning from my experiences with policy research.

Policy research is an important way to make a difference in this world. The policy research process is like an ocean voyage, with long, straight stretches (the activities in policy research phases) punctuated by occasional stays in port (policy research deliverables). But, unlike ocean voyages, the policy research process doesn't eventually come to an end. There are always new policy problems to tackle, new stakeholders to engage, new ways to synthesize and to collect new evidence, and new ways to communicate effectively with others. It's this constant refreshing that makes policy research an exciting, lifelong endeavor. Bon voyage!

References

African Medical and Research Foundation. (2006). Malaria prevention and control strategy, 2006–2010. Retrieved from http://www.amref.org/docs/malaria_strategy.pdf

Anderson, L. M., Shinn, C., Fullilove, M. T., Scrimshaw, S. C., Fielding, J. E., Normand, J., & Carande-Kulis, V. G. (2003). The effectiveness of early childhood development programs: A systematic review. *American Journal of Preventive Medicine, 24*(3S), 32–46.

Anechiarico, F., & Jacobs, J. B. (1995). Purging corruption from public contracting: The "solutions" are now part of the problem. *New York Law School Law Review, 40,* 143.

Bardach, E. (2009). *A practical guide to policy analysis: The eightfold path.* Washington, DC: CQ Press.

Beiser, V. (2011, May–June). Save the poor. Sell to them. *Miller-McCune,* pp. 46–56.

Bornstein, D., & Davis, S. (2010). *Social entrepreneurship: What everyone needs to know.* New York, NY: Oxford University Press.

Bourgois, P. (2002). *In search of respect: Selling crack in El Barrio.* Cambridge, UK: Cambridge University Press.

Braithwaite, J. (1979). Transnational corporations and corruption: Towards some international solutions. *International Journal of the Sociology of Law, 7,* 125–142.

Bristol, N. (2007, October 26). Battling HIV/AIDS: Should more money be spent on prevention? *CQ Researcher,* 17: 889–912. Retrieved from http://library.cqpress.com/cqresearcher/document.php?id=cqresrre2007102600

Culnan, M. J. (2011). Accountability as the basis for regulating privacy: Can information security regulations inform privacy policy? In *Future of privacy forum, privacy papers for policy makers 2011.* Retrieved from http://www.futureofprivacy.org/the-privacy-papers

Cummins, L. K., Byers, K. V., & Pedrick, L. (2011). Defining policy practice in social work: In *Policy practice for social workers: New strategies for a new era* (Rev. ed.). Boston, MA: Pearson Higher Education.

Drucker, P. F. (1985). *Implementation and entrepreneurship: Practice and principles.* New York, NY: Harper & Row.

Dwyer, T. (2006). Urban water policy: In need of economics. *Agenda, 13*(1), 3–16.

Federal Highway Administration. (2011, May 16). *Impact methodologies: Cost-benefit.* Retrieved from http://www.fhwa.dot.gov/planning/toolbox/costbenefit_forecasting.htm

Fichman, R. G., & Moses, S. A. (1999). An incremental process for software implementation. *Sloan Management Review, 40*(2), 39–52.

Florida, R. (2005). The world is spiky. *Atlantic Monthly, 296*(3), 48–51.

Hersh, W., Helfand, M., Wallace, J., Kraemer, D., Patterson, P., Shapiro, S., & Greenlick, M. (2002). A systematic review of the efficacy of telemedicine for making diagnostic and management decisions. *Journal of Telemedicine and Telecare, 8*(4), 197–209.

Hoque, B. A., Aziz, K., Hasan, S., & Patwary, M. (1991). Maintaining village water pumps by women volunteers in Bangladesh. *Health Policy and Planning, 6*(2), 176–180.

Intergovernmental Panel on Climate Change. (2012). *Reports*. Retrieved from http://
www.ipcc.ch/publications_and_data/publications_and_data_reports.shtml

Kahn, J. (2010, April 4). Bribe fighter: The strange but true tale of a phony currency,
shame, and a grass-roots movement that could go global. *Boston Globe.*

Kahneman, D. (2011). *Thinking, fast and slow*. New York, NY: Macmillan.

Keiser, J, Singer, B. H., & Utzinger, J. (2005). Reducing the burden of malaria in different
eco-epidemiological settings with environmental management: A systematic review.
The Lancet, 5(11), 695–708.

Koretz, D. (1982). Developing useful evaluation: A case history and some practical guidelines. In L. Saxe & D. Koretz (Eds.), *New directions for program evaluation* (No. 14).
San Francisco, CA: Jossey-Bass.

Leisinger, K. M. (1998). Multinational corporations, governance deficits, and corruption: Discussing a complex issue from the perspective of business ethics. In
H. Lange, A. Löhr, & H. Steinmann (Eds.), *Working across cultures: Ethical perspectives for intercultural management* (pp. 113–139). Boston, MA: Kluwer
Academic.

Lengler, C. (2004). Insecticide-treated bed nets and curtains for preventing malaria.
Cochrane Database of Systematic Reviews, 2, Article Number CD00363.

Lipton, D. (1992). How to maximize utilization of evaluation research by policy-
makers. *Annals of the American Academy of Political and Social Science,
521,* 175–188.

Lund, J. R., Hanak, E., Fleenor, W. E., Bennett, W. A., Howitt, R. E., Mount, J. F., &
Moyle, P. (2010). *Comparing futures for the Sacramento-San Joaquin Delta.*
Berkeley: University of California Press.

Luo, Y., Sun, J., & Wang, S. (2011). Emerging economy copycats: Capability, environment,
and strategy. *Academy of Management Perspectives, 25*(2), 37–56.

Mair, F., & Whitten, P. (2000). Systematic review of studies of patient satisfaction with
telemedicine. *British Journal of Medicine, 320,* 1517–1520.

McBride, R. (2011, May 25). *FDA data analysis reveals adverse drug combo.*
Retrieved from http://www.fiercebiotechit.com/story/fda-data-analysis-reveals-
adverse-drug-combo/2011-07-25

Mukherjee, A. (2008, April 1). Merry-go-round water pump to solve Africa's water problem.
Ecofriend: Green Living. Retrieved from http://www.ecofriend.com/entry/merri-go-
round-water-pump-to-solve-africas-water-problem

Mullins, J., & Komisar, R. (2009). *Getting to plan B: Breaking through to a better
business model.* Boston, MA: Harvard Business Press.

Munger, M.C. (2000). *Analyzing policy: choices, conflicts, and practices.* New York,
NY: W.W. Norton.

Nagel, S. S. (1984). *Contemporary public policy analysis.* Tuscaloosa: University of
Alabama Press.

Niemiec, R. M. (2010, September 22). *Vehicle for change.* Retrieved from http://
www.thebiggreenbus.org/blog/?m=201009

No need to panic about global warming. (2012, January 27). [Editorial]. *Wall Street
Journal.* Retrieved from http://online.wsj.com/

Nordhaus, W. (2012, March 22). Why the global warming skeptics are wrong. *New York Review of Books, LIV*(5), 32–34.

Pawson, R. (2006). *Evidence-based policy: A realist perspective.* London, UK: Sage.

Pearce, F. (2009, March 24). "Wasted" wells fail to solve Africa's water problems. *New Scientist.* Retrieved from http://www.newscientist.com/

Postel, S. (2001). Growing more food with less water. *Scientific American, 284*(2), 46–51.

Putre, L. (2011, Spring/Summer). Are we finally ready to cut the paper out of doctors' paperwork? *Case.edu Think,* pp. 28–33.

Reij, C. (1991). *Indigenous soil and water conservation in Africa* (Vol. Gatekeeper Series, No. 27). London, UK: International Institute for Environment and Development. Retrieved from http://pubs.iied.org/pdfs/6104IIED.pdf

Roan, S. (2011, June 13). Pregnant women show an amazing lack of knowledge about childbirth options, study shows. *Los Angeles Times.* Retrieved from http://www.latimes.com/

Roine, R., Ohinmaa, A., & Hailey, D. (2001). Assessing telemedicine: A systematic review of the literature. *Canadian Medical Association Journal, 165*(6), 763–771.

Sabatier, P. A. (Ed.). (2007). *Theories of the policy process* (2nd ed.). Boulder, CO: Westview.

Shadish, W. R., Cook, T. D., & Campbell, D. T. (2002). *Experimental and quasi-experimental designs for generalized causal inference.* Boston, MA: Houghton Mifflin.

Smith, A. G., & Robbins, A. E. (1982). Structured ethnography: The study of parental involvement. *American Behavioral Scientist, 26*(1), 45–61.

Stapenhurst, F., & Langseth, P. (1997). The role of the public administration in fighting corruption. *International Journal of Public Sector Management, 10*(5), 311–330.

Stone, D. (2012). *Policy paradox: The art of political decision making* (3rd ed.). New York, NY: W.W. Norton.

Thomson Reuters Accelus. (2011). *Anti-bribery and corruption: A special report—An increased burden on senior management.* Retrieved from http://www.anticorruption blog.com/Thomson%20Reuters%20-%20Anti-Bribery%20and%20Corruption %20-%20Special%20Report.pdf

UNICEF. (2012, February). *The state of the world's children 2012: Executive summary.* Retrieved from http://www.unicef.org/publications/files/SOWC_2012-Executive_ Summary_EN_13Mar2012.pdf

Whitten, P. S., Mair, F. S., Haycox, A., Mayt, C. R., Williams, T. L., & Hellmich, S. (2002). Systematic review of cost effectiveness studies of telemedicine interventions. *British Journal of Medicine, 324,* 1424–1437.

Index

Accidental policy researchers, 3–5,
    146–147
  advocacy role and, 4
  clients and, 4
  entrepreneurial role and, 4
  intrapreneurship and, 4
  methodological flexibility and, 4–5
  See also Policy research
Action-feedback-reaction cycle, 2–3
Activities:
  alternative intervention evaluation
    activity, 107, 109–112, 110 (table)
  alternative intervention generation
    activity, 100–107
  Base Case development activity,
    98–100
  Case for Change drafting activity,
    121–125, 122 (table),
    125–126 (tables)
  concept definition refinement activity,
    67–71, 71 (table)
  confidence-in-evidence assessment
    activity, 87–88
  conversing with/learning from
    stakeholders activity, 125–127,
    128 (table)
  data collection method selection
    activity, 76–84, 77 (table),
    80 (table), 85 (table)
  data type selection activity, 71–76,
    73–74 (table)
  ethical dilemma resolution activity,
    84, 86–87, 87 (table)
  evidence fragment synthesis activity,
    53–58, 54 (table), 56 (table)
  evidence syntheses identification/
    evaluation activity, 46–53,
    48–51 (tables)
  expert identification/engagement
    activity, 33

implementation alternatives
    generation/evaluation activity,
    112–114
  launch phase and, 15, 16 (figure),
    19–35
  message visibility activity, 127–129,
    129 (table)
  obtaining new evidence phase and,
    64 (figure), 67–88
  policy design recommendation phase
    and, 95 (figure), 97–114
  Policy Problem Change Wheel
    activity, 21–26, 22 (figure),
    26 (table)
  Policy Solution Change Wheel
    activity, 33–34, 35–36 (figures)
  research question framing activity,
    20–21
  resource-based decision process
    activity, 129–131, 132 (table)
  stakeholder analysis activity,
    29–32, 32 (figure)
  stakeholder engagement expansion
    phase and, 119 (figure), 120–132
  STORM context familiarization
    activity, 26–29, 28 (table)
  synthesizing evidence phase and,
    43 (figure), 45–58
Additional evidence. See Obtaining new
    evidence phase of policy research
Advisory role, 37–38
Advocacy role, 4, 118, 141–142
African Medical and Research
    Foundation, 52
After-action reviews, 144–145
Alternative interventions, 100–102,
    108 (table)
  analysis of, 5, 7, 13
  Big-Bang intervention, 102–103,
    108 (table)

complementary interventions,
105–107, 108 (table)
evaluation of, 107, 109–112,
110 (table)
generation of, 100–107
incremental interventions, 103–105,
108 (table)
See also Interventions
Amateur policy researchers.
See Accidental policy researchers
American National Election Studies,
73 (table)
Anechiarico, F., 107
Archival data, 72–74, 73–74 (table),
85 (table)
Association of Religion Data Archives,
73 (table)

Babbie, E. R., 65
Base Cases, 13, 98–100, 107, 109–111,
110 (table), 113, 115
Becker, H., 65
Benefit corporations, 4
Bennett, W. A., 100, 101
Best possible solutions, 6, 7, 8
Big-Bang interventions, 102–103,
108 (table), 114
Big Dig project, 78
Bloom, H. S., 65
Bourgois, P., 83
Brent, R. J., 65
Briggs, A. H., 65
Bristol, N., 34
Business data sources,
25, 27 (table), 47
Business entrepreneurship, 3, 14
See also Entrepreneurship; Social
entrepreneurship
Buy-in, 38
Byers, K. V., 118

Campbell, D. T., 65
Campbell Collaboration, 46, 48 (table)
Capacity to learn principle, 143–146

Case for Change messages, 117–118
audience personal experiences, ties
to, 123
elements in, 121
essential evidence, presentation of,
121–122, 122 (table)
initial message, drafting of, 121–125,
122 (table), 125–126 (tables)
mirroring technique, audience
cognitive needs and, 124–125,
125 (table)
numbers/stories in, 121
persuasion memo for, 132, 133 (table)
policy design recommendations,
credibility of, 122–123
See also Stakeholder engagement
expansion phase of policy
research
Case studies, 53–55, 54 (table), 82–83,
85 (table)
Center for Evidence-Based Crime
Policy (CEBCP), 48 (table)
Change process, 2–3, 14
change levers/malleable variables
and, 10
negative consequences, anticipation/
mitigation of, 5–6
policy research example and, 7–9
theory of the intervention and, 6
theory of the problem and, 6
turbulent environment for, 8–9
unintended consequences and, 9
See also Case for Change messages;
Interventions; Launch phase of
policy research; Policy decision
making; Policy research;
Stakeholder engagement
expansion phase of policy
research; Stakeholders
Channels for messages, 128, 129, 134
CIA World Factbook, 73 (table)
Clients, 4
Climate change policy, 1, 48, 75,
100, 131

Closed-ended questions, 81
Cochrane Collaboration in Healthcare,
    46–47, 48 (table)
Complementary interventions, 105–107,
    108 (table)
Compromise, 6–7, 32
Concept refinement, 67–68
    multiple indicators, utilization of,
        69–70
    operationalizing key concepts and,
        68–69, 71 (table)
    proxy/unobtrusive measures and,
        70–71
    See also Obtaining new evidence
        phase of policy research
Cook, T. D., 65
Corporate policy, ix
    corruption, coordinated interventions
        and, 105–107
    policy change, turbulent environment
        for, 8
    policy research example and, 7–9
    value conflicts, creative navigation
        of, 8
Cost-benefit analysis, 3, 5, 76–77,
    77 (table)
Cost-effectiveness analysis, 77–78,
    77 (table), 85 (table)
Creative approaches, 5, 7, 8, 9, 10
Creativity principle, 138–139
Credibility, 118, 120, 122–123,
    124, 142
Crowdsourcing options, 75
Cultural interventions, 107
Cummins, L. K., 118

Data collection, 25–26, 27 (table),
    33, 42
    archival data, 72–74, 73–74 (table),
        85 (table)
    case studies, 53–55, 54 (table),
        82–83, 85 (table)
    concepts, meaningful/measurable
        definition of, 67–71, 71 (table)

confidence-in-evidence assessment
    and, 87–88
cost-benefit analysis data, 76–77,
    77 (table)
cost-effectiveness analysis data,
    77–78, 77 (table), 85 (table)
crowdsourcing options and, 75
data collection method selection,
    76–84, 77 (table), 80 (table),
    85 (table)
documented new evidence memo
    and, 90–91 (table), 91
evidence collection design memo
    and, 89–90, 90 (table)
field experiments and, 78–80,
    80 (table), 85 (table)
interviews and, 80–81, 85 (table)
LOFE mind-set and, 75–76
Policy Change Wheels application
    and, 66
primary data, 71, 74–76
proxy/unobtrusive measures and,
    70–71
quasi-experiments and, 79
secondary data, 71–74, 73–74 (table)
social impact assessment data,
    78, 85 (table)
surveys/questionnaires and,
    79, 81–82, 85 (table)
systematic reviews, evidence
    syntheses and, 46–53,
    48–51 (tables)
See also Ethics issues; Obtaining
    new evidence phase of policy
    research; Synthesizing evidence
    phase of policy research
Decision documents. *See Policy design
    recommendation* design phase of
    policy research
Deliverables, 11
    advisory group deliverable,
        37–38
    Case for Change persuasion memo
        deliverable, 132, 133 (table)

communication/engagement plan
  deliverable, 132–134
documented new evidence memo
  deliverable, 90–91 (table), 91
documented synthesis deliverable, 59
evidence adequacy decision
  deliverable, 59–60
evidence collection design memo
  deliverable, 89–90, 90 (table)
launch phase and, 15, 16 (figure),
  35–38, 45–46
obtaining new evidence phase and,
  64 (figure), 88–91
policy decision document deliverable,
  115, 115–116 (table)
policy design recommendation
  phase and, 95 (figure),
  115, 115–116 (table)
reframed research question
  deliverable, 35, 37
stakeholder commitment to change
  deliverable, 134
stakeholder engagement expansion
  phase and, 119 (figure), 132–134
synthesizing evidence phase and,
  43 (figure), 59–60
Design of recommendations. See Policy
  design recommendation phase of
  policy research
Downstreamers, 147
Dwyer, T., 77

Economic models, 5
Education policy, 3, 10, 53, 70, 79
Education principle, 141–142
Electronic message media,
  128, 129, 134
Employment policy, 3
Entrepreneurship, 3
  accidental policy researchers and, 4
  intrapreneurship and, 4
  policy researcher role and, 7
Environmental policy, ix, 52, 66, 78, 131
EPPI Centre, 48 (table)

Ethics issues, 84, 87 (table)
  corruption, coordinated interventions
    and, 105–107
  data integrity and, 84
  do-no-harm principle and, 86
  identity information, collection/
    storage of, 84, 86
  outcomes, overpromises on, 86
  participants, results information/
    comments and, 86
  time, wasting of, 86–87
Evidence-based decision making, ix, 2
  best practices in, 47
  concept definition refinement and,
    67–71, 71 (table)
  conflicting proposals, compromise
    and, 6–7
  intervention design and, 3
  meaning, role of, 2, 6, 13
  policy research and, 2–3, 9
  syntheses of evidence and, 46–53,
    48–51 (tables)
  See also Obtaining new evidence
    phase of policy research;
    Synthesizing evidence phase of
    policy research
Evidence-Based Management site,
  48 (table)
Evidence for Policy and Practice
  Information, 48 (table)
Existing evidence. See Evidence-based
  decision making; Synthesizing
  evidence phase of policy research
Experiential learning, 3
Expert knowledge, 33

Federal Highway Administration
  (FHWA), 76
Feedback loops, 2–3, 143–146, 147
Field experiments, 78–80, 80 (table),
  85 (table)
Fleenor, W. E., 100, 101
Florida, R., 123
For-profit organizations, 4

Gallup polls, 73 (table)
General Social Survey (GSS), 73 (table)
Geographical information system
    (GIS), 72
Geospatial data, 74 (table)
Global Malaria Eradication
    Campaign, 52
Global warming policy, 20–21, 23,
    25, 26 (table), 31, 32 (figure)
Governmental data, 25, 27 (table)
Government corruption, 105–107

Hailey, D., 49
Hanak, E., 100, 101
Hands-on learning, 3
Haycox, A., 49
Head Start program, 21, 45, 53, 70
Health care policy, 3, 10, 34, 52,
    68–69, 99
Helfand, M., 49
Hellmich, S., 49
Hersh, W., 49
Homelessness policy, 21, 24, 25,
    26 (table)
Howitt, R. E., 100, 101

Identity information, 84, 86
Implementability, 19, 67–68, 112–114
Incremental interventions, 103–105,
    108 (table)
Indicators. *See* Tracking indicators
Intergovernmental Panel on Climate
    Change (IPCC), 131
Internet message media, 128, 129, 134
Interuniversity Consortium for Political
    and Social Research (ICPSR),
    74 (table)
Interventions, 3, 33
    best possible solutions and, 6, 7, 8
    Big-Bang interventions, 102–103,
        108 (table), 114
    case example of, 7–9
    complementary interventions,
        105–107, 108 (table)

cost-benefit analyses and, 3, 5
creative approach to, 10
cultural compatibility and, 99
cultural interventions, 107
fragments-of-evidence analytical
    approach and, 55–58, 56 (table)
geographic settings and, 66
implementability of, 19, 67–68,
    112–114
incremental interventions, 103–105,
    108 (table), 114
inflexible interventions, adverse
    effects of, 106–107
intrapreneurship and, 4
malleable variables/change levers
    and, 10
MECE interventions, 101–102
multi-pronged approach and, 10
negative consequences, anticipation/
    mitigation of, 5–6
pilot programs and, 78–79, 96
policy decision document and, 115,
    115–116 (table)
recommendations for, 8, 10
results-driven incrementalism
    approach to, 114
stakeholders in, 8, 10, 11, 13, 14
theory of the intervention and, 6, 10
treatment fidelity assessment and, 89
unintended consequences and, 8–9,
    66, 106–107
See also Alternative interventions;
    Change process;
    Entrepreneurship; Obtaining
    new evidence phase of policy
    research; Policy decision
    making; Policy design
    recommendation phase of policy
    research; Policy research; Policy
    Solution Change Wheel
    framework
Interviews, 80–81, 85 (table)
Intrapreneurship, 4
Iterative process principle, 140–141

Jacobs, J. B., 107
Journalist's Resource, 48 (table)

Kahn, J., 104
Knowledge dissemination principle,
    146–147
Knowledge makers, vii
  best possible solutions and, 6–7
  downstreamers and, 147
  expert knowledge and, 33
  feedback loops and, 143–146
  knowledge dissemination and, 146–147
  tacit knowledge and, 147
  See also Evidence-based decision
    making; Obtaining new evidence
    phase of policy research; Policy
    research; Policy research
    voyage; Synthesizing evidence
    phase of policy research
Kolenikov, S., 65
Koretz, D., 124
Kraemer, D., 49

Langseth, P., 105
Launch phase of policy research,
    11, 15, 16 (figure)
  activities for, 15, 16 (figure), 19–35
  advisory group deliverable and,
    37–38
  data collection sources and, 25–26,
    27 (table)
  deliverables of, 15, 16 (figure),
    35–38, 45–46
  expert identification/engagement
    activity and, 33
  initial policy solution options and,
    33–34, 35 (figure)
  manageability indicator and,
    18, 20–21
  meaningfulness indicator and,
    17, 18, 21
  Policy Problem Change Wheel
    activity and, 21–26, 22 (figure),
    26 (table)

Policy Solution Change Wheel
    activity and, 33–34,
    35–36 (figures)
  reframed research question
    deliverable and, 35, 37
  research question development
    and, 18
  research question framing activity
    and, 20–21
  stakeholder analysis activity and,
    29–32, 32 (figure)
  stakeholder engagement indicator
    and, 18–19
  STORM context familiarization
    activity and, 26–29, 28 (table)
  tracking indicators for, 17–19
  See also Change process; Policy
    research; Synthesizing evidence
    phase of policy research
Learning-by-doing, 3
Leisinger, K. M., 105
Lessons-learned reviews, 145–146
Lipton, D., 124
Literature review, 46–53, 48–51 (tables)
LOFE (leverage/optimism/focus/
    enthusiasm) mind-set, 75–76
Lund, J. R., 100, 101

Mair, F. S., 49
Malleable variables, 10
Manageability indicator, 18, 20–21,
    96–97
Mayt, C. R., 49
Meaning, 2, 6, 13
  concepts, meaningful definition of,
    67–71, 71 (table)
  meaningfulness indicator, 17, 18, 21,
    94, 96
MECE (Mutually Exclusive and
    Collectively Exhaustive)
    interventions, 101–102, 112
Mechanical Turk app, 75
Megan's Law evaluation, 55–56,
    56 (table)

Military policy, 79–80, 80 (table),
   90–91 (tables)
Mirroring technique, 124–125,
   125 (table)
Mount, J. F., 100, 101
Munger, M. C., 65
Myers, M., 65

New evidence. *See* Obtaining new
   evidence phase of policy research
Nongovernmental organizations
   (NGOs), 3, 25, 27 (table)
Nonprofit organizations, ix, 4

Obtaining new evidence phase of policy
   research, 63–65, 64 (figure)
   activities for, 64 (figure), 67–88
   archival data sources and, 72–74,
      73–74 (table), 85 (table)
   case studies and, 82–83, 85 (table)
   concept definition refinement activity
      and, 67–71, 71 (table)
   confidence-in-evidence assessment
      activity and, 87–88
   cost-benefit analysis approach and,
      76–77, 77 (table)
   cost-effectiveness analysis approach
      and, 77–78, 77 (table), 85 (table)
   data collection method selection
      activity and, 76–84, 77 (table),
      80 (table), 85 (table)
   data type selection decision activity
      and, 71–76, 73–74 (table)
   deliverables of, 64 (figure), 88–91
   documented new evidence
      memo deliverable and,
      90–91 (table), 91
   ethical dilemma resolution activity
      and, 84, 86–87, 87 (table)
   evidence collection design memo,
      89–90, 90–91 (tables)
   feedback mechanisms and, 147
   field experiments and, 78–80,
      80 (table), 85 (table)

flexible research question focus
      indicator and, 66–67
   interviews and, 80–81, 85 (table)
   LOFE mind-set and, 75–76
   multiple indicators, utilization
      of, 69–70
   operationalizing key concepts and,
      68–69, 71 (table)
   Policy Change Wheels application
      indicator and, 66
   primary data collection and,
      71, 74–76
   proxy/unobtrusive measures
      and, 70–71
   quasi-experiments and, 79
   research design literature and,
      65, 65 (table)
   secondary data collection and, 71–74,
      73–74 (table)
   social impact assessment and,
      78, 85 (table)
   surveys/questionnaires and,
      79, 81–82, 85 (table)
   tracking indicators for, 66–67
   See also Evidence-based decision
      making; Policy research;
      Synthesizing evidence phase of
      policy research
Ohinmaa, A., 49
Open-ended questions, 81
Operationalized concepts,
   68–71, 71 (table)

Patterson, P., 49
Pedrick, L., 118
Pfeffer, J., 48
Pilot programs, 78–79, 96
Policy decision document,
   115, 115–116 (table)
Policy decision making, vii, ix, 14
   action-feedback-reaction cycle
      and, 2–3
   best possible solutions and, 6, 7, 8
   case example of, 7–9

consensus of opinion, best possible
      solutions and, 6, 7, 8
evidence-based decisions and, ix, 2, 3
negative consequences, anticipation/
      mitigation of, 5–6, 14
rational choice theory and, 6, 8
recommendations for policy and, 8
turbulent environment for, 8–9
unintended consequences and, 9, 14
value conflicts, navigation of, 8, 9
See also Change process;
      Interventions; Launch phase of
      policy research; Policy design
      recommendation phase of policy
      research; Policy research;
      Stakeholders; Synthesizing
      evidence phase of policy
      research
Policy design recommendation phase
      of policy research, 8–9, 10, 13,
      93–94, 95 (figure)
activities for, 95 (figure), 97–114
alternative intervention evaluation
      activity and, 107, 109–112,
      110 (table)
alternative intervention generation
      activity and, 100–107,
      108 (table)
Base Case development activity and,
      98–100
Big-Bang interventions and,
      102–103, 108 (table)
complementary interventions and,
      105–107, 108 (table)
corruption, coordinated interventions
      and, 105–107
cultural interventions and, 107
deliverables of, 95 (figure),
      114–116
implementation alternatives
      generation/evaluation activity
      and, 112–114
incremental interventions and,
      103–105, 108 (table)

inflexible interventions, adverse
      effects of, 106–107
manageable choices indicator and,
      96–97
meaningful choices indicator and,
      94, 96
MECE interventions and, 101–102
policy decision document and,
      115, 115–116 (table)
results-driven incrementalism
      approach and, 114
stakeholder beliefs/preferences
      and, 94
tracking indicators for, 94, 96–97
unintended consequences and, 98,
      106–107, 111–112
wait/monitor recommendation
      and, 98
See also Obtaining new evidence
      phase of policy research; Policy
      research; Synthesizing evidence
      phase of policy research
Policy position commitment principle,
      142–143
Policy Problem Change Wheel
      framework, ix, 10, 11, 15,
      21–22, 22 (figure)
content alignment analysis and, 39
data collection sources and,
      25–26, 27 (table), 33
how question/causal model
      and, 23–24
mechanisms of policy problems and, 24
obtaining new evidence phase and, 66
outcome improvements, expectations
      for, 24
what not question and, 23
what question and, 23
who/where questions and, 23, 26–27
why not question and, 25
why question and, 24
See also Launch phase of policy
      research; Policy Solution
      Change Wheel framework

Policy research, 1–2
  accidental/amateur policy researchers
    and, 3–5
  action-feedback-reaction cycle
    and, 3
  alternative interventions and, 5, 7, 13
  base case description and, 13
  case example of, 7–9
  change process and, 2–3, 7–9
  clients of, 4
  context of, 6–9
  cost-benefit analyses and, 5
  creative approaches in, 10, 13
  definition of, 2–3, 9
  discredited/devalued research and, 9
  evidence-based research and, 2, 3, 9
  evidence examination and, 11, 13
  intervention design and, 3, 5, 10
  key characteristics of, 9–11
  literature review on, 65, 65 (table)
  negative consequences, anticipation/
    mitigation of, 5–6, 14
  practitioners of, 3–5
  process voyage in, 11–13, 12 (figure)
  professionalization of, 5
  professional policy researchers and,
    3, 4–5
  rational choice theory and, 6, 8, 9
  recommendations for policy and,
    8–9, 10, 13
  research questions in, 9–10,
    11, 13, 18
  responsible research practices and,
    5–6, 8–9
  secondary analysis methodology and,
    4–5, 13
  theory of the intervention and, 6, 10
  theory of the problem and, 6, 10
  See also Launch phase of policy
    research; Obtaining new
    evidence phase of policy
    research; Policy decision
    making; Policy design
    recommendation phase of policy

research; Policy research
    voyage; Stakeholder engagement
    expansion phase of policy
    research; Synthesizing evidence
    phase of policy research
Policy research voyage, 11–13,
    12 (figure), 137–138
  capacity to learn principle and,
    143–146
  creativity principle and, 138–139
  education principle and, 141–142
  iterative process principle and,
    140–141
  knowledge dissemination principle
    and, 146–147
  launch phase and, 16 (figure)
  obtaining new evidence phase and,
    64 (figure)
  policy position commitment principle
    and, 142–143
  policy design recommendation phase
    and, 95 (figure)
  principles of, 138–147
  responsibility principle and, 140
  stakeholder engagement expansion
    phase and, 119 (figure)
  synthesizing evidence phase and,
    43 (figure)
  See also Policy research
Policy Solution Change Wheel
    framework, 22, 24, 33–34,
    35–36 (figures), 39
  case study evidence evaluation and,
    53–55, 54 (table)
  obtaining new evidence phase
    and, 66
  See also Policy Problem Change
    Wheel framework; Policy
    research
Primary data collection, 71, 74–76
Problems. *See* Interventions; Policy
    Problem Change Wheel
    framework; Policy research; Policy
    Solution Change Wheel framework

Process of research. *See* Policy
 research voyage
Professional policy researchers, 3, 4–5
Proxy measures, 70–71

Quasi-experiments, 79
Questionnaires, 79, 81–82, 85 (table)
Questions. *See* Research questions

Rational choice theory, 6, 8, 9
Recommendations. *See* Policy design
 recommendation phase of policy
 research; Policy research
Research questions, 9–10, 11, 13
 flexible research questions, 66–67
 framing research questions, 20–21
 meaningfulness indicator and, 18
Research voyage. *See* Policy
 research voyage
Resource distribution, viii, 18
Responsibility principle, 140
Responsible research practices, 5–6
Results-driven incrementalism
 approach, 114
Roan, S., 82
Robbins, A. E., 124
Roine, R., 49

Secondary analysis methodology, 4–5, 13
Secondary data collection, 71–74,
 73–74 (table)
Shadish, W. R., 65
Shapiro, S., 49
Smith, A. G., 124
Social entrepreneurship, 3, 14
 accidental policy researchers and, 4
 See also Business entrepreneurship;
 Entrepreneurship
Social impact assessment, 78, 85 (table)
Social media networks, 128, 129
Social/technical/organizational/
 regulatory/market (STORM)
 context, ix, 10, 11, 15, 27–29,
 28 (table), 34, 39

Solutions. *See* Interventions; Policy
 Solution Change Wheel framework
Stakeholder Analysis tool, 11, 15,
 29–32, 32 (figure), 39
Stakeholder engagement expansion
 phase of policy research,
 13, 117–118, 119 (figure)
 activities for, 119 (figure), 120–132
 advocacy role and, 118
 Case for Change drafting activity
 and, 121–125, 122 (table),
 125–126 (tables)
 Case for Change messages and,
 117–118
 Case for Change persuasion memo
 deliverable, 132, 133 (table)
 communication/engagement plan
 deliverable and, 132–134
 conversing with/learning from
 stakeholders activity and,
 125–127, 128 (table)
 credibility indicator and, 118, 120,
 122–123, 124
 deliverables of, 119 (figure), 132–134
 message freshness and, 130–131
 message visibility activity,
 127–129, 129 (table)
 mirroring technique, audience
 cognitive needs and, 124–125,
 125 (table)
 resource-based decision process
 activity and, 129–131,
 132 (table)
 stakeholder commitment to change
 deliverable, 134
 touch points for messages and,
 128–129, 129 (table), 130–131
 tracking indicators for, 118, 120
 understandability indicator and,
 118, 120, 123–125, 125 (table)
 See also Policy research;
 Stakeholders
Stakeholders, 8, 10, 11, 14
 advisory role and, 37–38

beliefs/preferences of, 94
buy-in and, 38
common ground focus and, 31, 32
definition of, 18, 29
disengagement of, 19
engagement of, 13, 18–19, 30
identification of, 29–30
implementability of solutions and, 19
multiple indicators, utilization of,
    69–70
stakeholder agreement, assessment
    of, 31, 32 (figure)
See also Stakeholder Analysis tool;
    Stakeholder engagement
    expansion phase of policy
    research
Stapenhurst, F., 105
Steinley, D., 65
STORM. *See* Social/technical/
    organizational/regulatory/market
    (STORM) context
Surveys, 79, 81–82, 85 (table)
Sutton, B., 48
Syntheses of evidence, 46–53,
    48–51 (tables)
Synthesizing evidence phase of policy
    research, 25, 41–42, 43 (figure)
activities for, 43 (figure), 45–58
data sources for, 42, 44
deliverables of, 43 (figure), 59–60
documented synthesis deliverable
    and, 59
evidence adequacy decision
    deliverable and, 59–60
evidence fragment synthesis activity
    and, 53–58, 54 (table), 56 (table)
evidence strength assessment
    indicator and, 44–45,
    58, 58 (table)
evidence syntheses identification/
    evaluation activity and, 46–53,
    48–51 (tables)
fragments-of-evidence analytical
    approach and, 55–58, 56 (table)

knowledge of evidence indicator and,
    42–44
launch phase deliverables and,
    45–46
quality/relevance of evidence and, 42,
    44, 57–58, 58 (table)
tracking indicators for, 42–45
See also Launch phase of policy
    research; Obtaining new
    evidence phase of policy
    research; Policy research
Systematic reviews, 46–53,
    48–51 (tables)

Tacit knowledge, 147
Theory of the intervention, 6, 10
Theory of the problem, 6, 10
Think tanks, 3
Thombs, L. A., 65
Touch points, 128–129, 129 (table),
    130–131
Tracking indicators, 11
credibility, 118, 120
evidence strength assessment,
    44–45, 58, 58 (table)
flexible research question focus,
    66–67
knowledge of evidence, 42–44
launch phase and, 17–19
manageability, 18, 96–97
meaningfulness, 17, 94, 96
obtaining new evidence phase and,
    66–67
Policy Change Wheels
    application, 66
policy design recommendation phase
    and, 94, 96–97
stakeholder engagement, 18–19
stakeholder engagement expansion
    phase and, 118, 120
synthesizing existing evidence phase
    and, 42–45
understandability, 118, 120
Treatment fidelity assessment, 89

U.S. Bureau of Labor Statistics, 73 (table)
U.S. Census Bureau data, 71–72
Understandability, 118, 120, 123–125, 125 (table)
Unintended consequences, 9, 14, 106–107, 111–112
United Nations Children's Fund (UNICEF), 129
Unobtrusive measures, 70–71

Validity assessment, 87–88
Value conflicts, 8
Vanclay, F., 65
Vartanian, T. P., 65
Voyage metaphor. *See* Policy research voyage

Wallace, J., 49
Water supply policy, 77–78, 77 (table), 100, 109, 110 (table)
Wheel frameworks. *See* Policy Problem Change Wheel framework; Policy Solution Change Wheel framework
White papers, 25, 27 (table), 128
Whitten, P. S., 49
Willan, A. R., 65
Williams, T. L., 49
Woodside, A. G., 65
The World Bank Data, 73 (table)

Yin, R. K., 65

⑤SAGE research**methods**

The essential online tool for researchers from the world's leading methods publisher

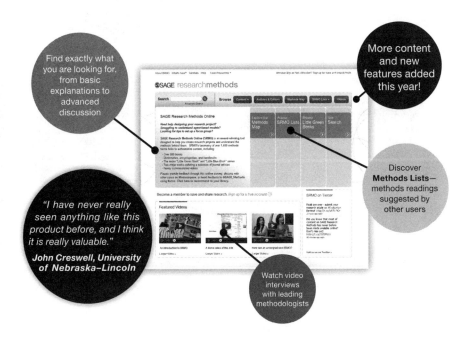

Find exactly what you are looking for, from basic explanations to advanced discussion

More content and new features added this year!

Discover **Methods Lists**— methods readings suggested by other users

"I have never really seen anything like this product before, and I think it is really valuable."

John Creswell, University of Nebraska–Lincoln

Watch video interviews with leading methodologists

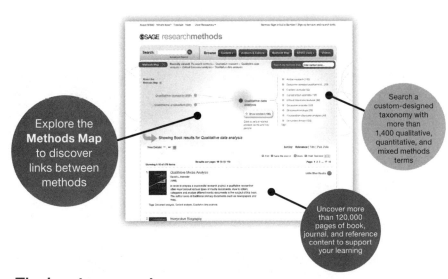

Explore the **Methods Map** to discover links between methods

Search a custom-designed taxonomy with more than 1,400 qualitative, quantitative, and mixed methods terms

Uncover more than 120,000 pages of book, journal, and reference content to support your learning

Find out more at
www.sageresearchmethods.com